Debbie Bliss
Toy Knits

Debbie Bliss
ToyKnits

More than 30 irresistible and easy-to-knit patterns

St. Martin's Griffin

New York

This book is for William and Eleanor.

Library of Congress Cataloging-in-Publication Data
Bliss, Debbie
   Toy Knits: more than 30 irresistible and
   easy-to-knit patterns
Debbie Bliss
   p. cm.
ISBN 0-312-11901-1
1. Knitting Patterns. 2. Soft toy making. I. Title.
TT 829.B55   1995
745.592'4   dc20
                                  95–1007
                                     CIP

First St. Martin's Griffin Edition: 1995
10 9 8 7 6 5 4 3

First published in the United Kingdom in 1995 by Ebury Press, Random House, 20 Vauxhall Bridge Road, London SW1V 2SA

Photography by Sandra Lane
Designed by Jerry Goldie
Styling by Marie Willey

Typeset by Textype Typesetters, Cambridge
Printed and bound in Singapore by Tien Wah Press

ALSO BY DEBBIE BLISS
New Baby Knits
Kid's Country Knits
Baby Knits
Kids' Knits for Heads, Hands, and Toes
Debbie Bliss Nursery Knits

The publishers would like to thank Old Town, 32 Elm Hill, Norwich, NR3 1HG (tel 01603 628100) for kindly lending props for photography.

Contents

Introduction

Toy Knits has been enormous fun to work on and I was delighted to be given this opportunity to put together a collection of over 40 knitted toys.

There are floppy-eared rabbits, fairytale mice, an elephant that skates and teddies, of course, from the tiny to the tartan. There are toys to cuddle and toys to dress, a Christmas angel and reindeer which I hope will be brought out year after year, and, as children love to use their own imagination, a patchwork farm complete with animals, hedges and fences, for them to create a landscape of their own.

Along the way I have had invaluable help from my children, William and Eleanor, who cast a critical or admiring eye over every completed idea, but this book would not have been possible without the assistance of Tina Egleton, my pattern checker, who came to my aid whenever my technical ability lagged behind my creative inspiration and who gave me unflagging practical support throughout the entire project.

Debbie Bliss

Basic Information

Safety

It is very important that a toy is suitable for the age of the child for whom it is intended. **Children under 3 years of age must never be given a toy that has any added extras such as eyes, buttons or felt.** All the toys in this book can be adapted if necessary to meet these requirements. The Bull, for example, does not have to have a nose ring; or the reins and the blanket could be omitted from the Camel and his eyes can be embroidered rather than sewn on. If a pipe cleaner is used, as in the Skating Elephant, make sure that it is well-contained within the stuffing and that it will not work through to the outside. Coloured plastic-headed pins should be used so that they can be easily seen and not inadvertently left in the toy. In general, make sure that any toys given to the very young have all limbs and any accessories such as hats and shoes securely sewn in place.

Tension

Tension is not as crucial when knitting toys as it would be for other knitted garments. Remember that a tighter or looser tension will produce a smaller or larger toy than that shown in the photograph, and that a loose tension will produce a more open fabric through which the stuffing will show.

Yarns

As long as the tension is the same as that given in the pattern, you can substitute yarns. As the yarn amounts are small, particularly for tiny garments, you will probably have oddments of yarn that you will be pleased to use up. All yarn amounts quoted are approximate.

Stuffing

Washable stuffing, which conforms to safety standards, should always be used.
Overstuffing can stretch the fabric so that the stuffing will show through, and if garter stitch has been used the knitting may become elongated. Understuffing can make the toy too floppy. This may be desirable in some toys, such as the Farmer Rabbits, when the bodies and limbs need to be soft and pliable. Others, however, such as the Camel and Reindeer, need to be stuffed extremely firmly to make them stand up.

Very small pieces, such as the reindeer antlers and the mice, should be stuffed as they are sewn up as it is impossible to stuff them afterwards.

Watch out for 'lumps' when stuffing. Tear the edges of each piece of stuffing so that when the next piece is inserted the edges blend in.

Abbreviations

alt=alternate
beg=begin(ning)
cont=continue
dec=decreas(e)ing
foll=following
inc=increas(e)ing
k=knit
m1=make one by picking up loop lying between st just worked and next st and work into the back of it
patt=pattern
p=purl
psso=pass slipped stitch over
rem=remain(ing)
rep=repeat
sl=slip
skpo=slip 1, k1, pass slipped st over
st(s)=stitch(es)
st st=stocking stitch
tbl=through back of loop(s)
tog=together
yb=yarn back
yf=yarn forward
yon=yarn over needle
yrn=yarn round needle

11
**Large Teddy
in Sailor Outfit**
SEE PAGE
40

13
Sailor Doll
SEE PAGE
43

15
*Small Rabbit
with Sweater*
SEE PAGE
46

16/17
Farm Play Mat
SEE PAGE
47

18
**Pig
and Piglets**
SEE PAGE
51

19
Sheep
SEE PAGE
49

Cow and Bull

SEE PAGE

52

25
Girl Rabbit
SEE PAGE
57

Teddy Bear with Fair Isle Slipover

SEE PAGE
65

Tartan Bear

SEE PAGE
64

32
Angel Rabbit
SEE PAGE
66

33
Skating Elephant
SEE PAGE
67

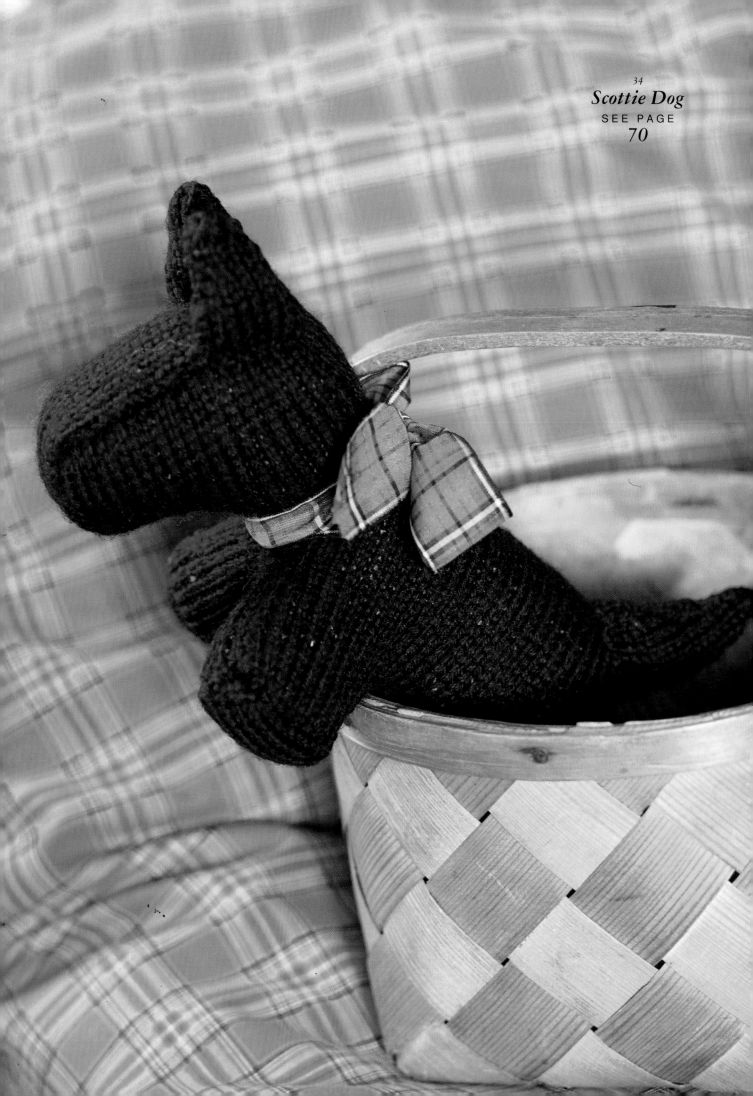

35
Dalmatian Dog
SEE PAGE
68

39
Camel
SEE PAGE
76

Large Teddy Bear in Sailor Outfit

See Page
11

Teddy Bear

RIGHT LEG
With A, cast on 26 sts. K 1 row.
Next row K1, [m1, k2] to last st, m1, k1. K 1 row.
Next row K5, [m1, k2] 5 times, k10, [m1, k2] 5 times, k4. K 1 row.
Next row K6, [m1, k3] 5 times, k9, [m1, k3] 5 times, k4. 59 sts. K 15 rows. **
Next row K12, [skpo] 3 times, [k2 tog] 3 times, k35. K 1 row.
Next row K9, [skpo] 3 times, [k2 tog] 3 times, k17, skpo, [k2 tog] twice, k9. K 1 row.
Next row K8, [skpo] twice, [k2 tog] twice, k28. 40 sts.
*** Cont in garter st, inc one st at each end of 6th row and 3 foll 4th rows. 48 sts. K 12 rows.
Next row K9, k2 tog, k2, skpo, k18, k2 tog, k2, skpo, k9. K 3 rows.
Next row K8, k2 tog, k2, skpo, k16, k2 tog, k2, skpo, k8. K 1 row.
Next row K7, k2 tog, k2, skpo, k14, k2

tog, k2, skpo, k7.
Cont in this way, dec 4 sts as set on 4 foll alt rows. 20 sts. K 1 row.
Cast off.
Join top, inner leg and sole seam, leaving an opening. Stuff firmly and close opening.

LEFT LEG
Work as given for Right Leg to **.
Next row K35, [skpo] 3 times, [k2 tog] 3 times, k12. K 1 row.
Next row K9, [skpo] twice, k2 tog, k17, [skpo] 3 times, [k2 tog] 3 times, k9. K 1 row.
Next row K28, [skpo] twice, [k2 tog] twice, k8. 40 sts.
Complete as given for Right Leg from *** to end.

BODY
Begin at neck edge.
With A, cast on 17 sts. K 1 row.
Next row [K twice in next st] to end. 34 sts. K 1 row.
Next row K4, [k twice in next st] to last 4 sts, k4. 60 sts. K 15 rows.
Next row K13, [k twice in next st] 4 times, k26, [k twice in next st] 4 times, k13. K 3 rows.
Next row K14, [k twice in next st, k1, k twice in next st] twice, k28, [k twice in next st, k1, k twice in next st] twice, k14. K 3 rows.
Next row K16, [k twice in next st, k1] 4 times, k29, [k twice in next st, k1] 4 times, k15. K 3 rows.
Next row K17, [k twice in next st, k2, k twice in next st, k1] twice, k31, [k twice in next st, k2, k twice in next st, k1] twice, k16. 92 sts. K 37 rows.
Next row K17, [skpo, k2, skpo, k1] twice, k31, [k2 tog, k2, k2 tog, k1] twice, k16. K 3 rows.
Next row K16, [skpo, k1] 4 times, k29, [k2 tog, k1] 4 times, k15. K 3 rows.
Next row K14, [skpo, k1, skpo] twice, k28, [k2 tog, k1, k2 tog] twice, k14.
* **Next 2 rows** K12, sl 1, yf, turn, sl 1, k12. K 1 row. *
Rep from * to * twice, then work the 2 turning rows again.
Next row K13, [skpo] 4 times, k26, [k2 tog] 4 times, k13.
Rep from * to * once, then work the 2 turning rows again.
Next row K12, [skpo] 4 times, k20, [k2 tog] 4 times, k12. K 1 row.
Next row K10, [skpo] 4 times, k16, [k2 tog] 4 times, k10. K 1 row.
Next row K8, [skpo] 4 times, k12, [k2 tog] 4 times, k8.
Next row [K2 tog] to end. 18 sts.
Cast off.

ARMS (make 2)
With A, cast on 7 sts. K 1 row.
Next row K1, [m1, k1] to end.
Rep last 2 rows once. 25 sts. K 1 row.
Next row K6, m1, k1, m1, k11, m1, k1, m1, k6. K 1 row.
Next row K7, m1, k1, m1, k13, m1, k1, m1, k7. K 1 row.
Next row K8, m1, k1, m1, k15, m1, k1, m1, k8. 37 sts. K 10 rows.
Next row K1, [k2 tog, k2] to end. 28 sts. K 3 rows.
Next row K1, [m1, k3] to end. 37 sts.
Cont in garter st, inc one st at each end of 3rd row and 3 foll 4th rows. 45 sts. K 16 rows.
Next row K8, k2 tog, k2, skpo, k17, k2 tog, k2, skpo, k8. K 3 rows.
Next row K7, k2 tog, k2, skpo, k15, k2 tog, k2, skpo, k7. K 1 row.
Next row K6, k2 tog, k2, skpo, k13, k2 tog, k2, skpo, k6.
Cont in this way, dec 4 sts as set on 4 foll alt rows. 17 sts. K 1 row. Cast off.
Join top and underarm seam, leaving an opening. Stuff firmly and close opening.

HEAD
Begin at snout.
With A, cast on 8 sts. K 1 row.
Next row K1, [m1, k1] to end.
Rep last 2 rows once more. 29 sts.
5th and every foll alt row K.
6th row K1, [m1, k13, m1, k1] twice.
8th row K1, [m1, k15, m1, k1] twice.
10th row K1, m1, k16, m1, k3, m1, k16, m1, k1.
12th row K1, m1, k17, m1, k5, m1, k17, m1, k1.
14th row K1, m1, k18, m1, k7, m1, k18, m1, k1.
16th row K1, m1, k19, m1, k9, m1, k19, m1, k1. 53 sts.
17th and 18 rows K.
19th row K2, [skpo, k1] 7 times, k8, [k2 tog, k1] 7 times, k1.
20th row K7, [m1, k4] 3 times, k1, [k4, m1] 3 times, k7. K 3 rows.
24th row K7, [m1, k5] 3 times, k1, [k5, m1] 3 times, k7. K 3 rows.
28th row K7, [m1, k6] 3 times, k1, [k6, m1] 3 times, k7. K 3 rows.
Cont in this way, inc 6 sts as set on next row and 3 foll alt rows. 81 sts. K 1 row.
Next row K5, [m1, k4] 7 times, k15, [k4, m1] 7 times, k5. 95 sts. K 20 rows.
Next row [K10, k2 tog] 7 times, k11. K 3 rows.
Next row [K9, k2 tog] 8 times. K 3 rows.
Next row [K8, k2 tog] 8 times. K 3 rows.
Next row [K7, k2 tog] 8 times. K 3 rows.
Cont in this way, dec 8 sts as set on next row and 5 foll alt rows. 16 sts. K 1 row.
Next row [K2 tog] 8 times.

Break off yarn. Thread end through rem sts, pull up and secure. Join seam, leaving an opening. Stuff firmly and close opening.

EARS (make 2)
With A, cast on 5 sts. K 1 row.
Next row K1, [m1, k1] to end. K 1 row.
Next row K1, [m1, k3, m1, k1] twice. K 1 row.
Next row K1, m1, k4, m1, k3, m1, k4, m1, k1. K 1 row.
Next row K1, m1, [k5, m1] 3 times, k1. 21 sts. K 15 rows.
Next row K1, skpo, k3, skpo, k5, k2 tog, k3, k2 tog, k1. K 1 row.
Next row K1, skpo, k2, skpo, k3, k2 tog, k2, k2 tog, k1. K 1 row.
Next row K1, [skpo, k1] twice, [k2 tog, k1] twice. K 1 row.
Next row K1, skpo, sl 1, k2 tog, psso, k2 tog, k1.
Cast off.

NOSE
With B, cast on 9 sts. K 3 rows.
Next row K1, skpo, k3, k2 tog, k1.
K 1 row.
Next row K1, skpo, k1, k2 tog, k1.
K 1 row.
Next row K1, sl 1, k2 tog, psso, k1.
K 1 row. K 3 tog and fasten off.

TO MAKE UP
Fold sides of body to centre, then join cast off edge. Gather neck edge of body, pull up and secure. Join back seam of body, leaving an opening. Stuff firmly and close opening. Sew head in position, placing back seam of head in line with back seam of body and underchin seam of head at centre of front of body. Sew on nose. Fold ears in half widthwise and stitch together open edge. Sew ears in place. With Black, embroider mouth and eyes. Attach yarn at seam about 1cm/¼in below top of one arm, thread through body at shoulder position, then attach other arm, pull up yarn tightly and thread through body again in same place, then attach to first arm again and fasten off. Attach legs at lower edge of body in same way as arms.

Sweater

BACK
With A, cast on 49 sts. K 7 rows.
Next row (right side) K7, m1, [k12, m1] 3 times, k6. 53 sts.
Next row K3, p47, k3.
Next row K.
Rep last 2 rows twice more. Beg with a p row, work in st st until Back measures 16cm/6¼in from beg, ending with a p row.
Shape Neck
Next row K18, cast off next 17 sts, k to end.
Work on last set of sts only. Dec one st at neck edge on next 5 rows. Cast off rem 13 sts.
With wrong side facing, rejoin yarn to rem sts and complete to match first side.

FRONT
Work as given for Back until Front measures 6cm/2¼in from beg, ending with a k row.
Next row P24, k5, p24.
Next row K.
Rep last 2 rows once more, then work first of the 2 rows again.
Next row K26, turn.
Work on this set of sts only.
Next row K2, p to end.
Next row K.
Rep last 2 rows until Front measures 11cm/4¼in from beg, ending at centre.
Shape Neck
Cast off 4 sts at beg of next row. Dec one st at neck edge on every right side row until 13 sts rem. Work few rows straight until Front matches Back to cast off edge, ending with a p row. Cast off.
With right side facing, rejoin yarn to rem sts, cast off 1, k to end.
Next row P to last 2 sts, k2.
Next row K.
Complete to match first side.

SLEEVES
With A, cast on 44 sts. K 7 rows.
Next row (right side) K4, m1, [k12, m1] 3 times, k4. 48 sts.
Beg with a p row, work in st st, inc one st at each end of 3 foll 3rd rows. 54 sts.
Work 5 rows straight. Cast off.

COLLAR
With B, cast on 41 sts.
1st row (right side) K1, [p1, k1] to end.

Change to C.
2nd row P1, [k1, p1] to end.
Rib 1 row, dec one st at each end.
Change to B and rib 2 rows, dec one st at each end of 2nd row. Change to C and rep last 2 rows once. 35 sts.
Cont in B only. Rib 1 row.
Beg with a k row, work in st st until Collar measures 10cm/4in from beg, ending with a p row.
Shape Neck
Next row K11, cast off next 13 sts, k to end.
Work on last set of sts only for left front side. Dec one st at inside edge on every 3rd row until 2 sts rem. Work 2 tog and fasten off.
With wrong side facing, rejoin yarn to rem sts and complete to match first side.

COLLAR EDGING
With B and right side facing, pick up and k45 sts evenly along left side edge of collar omitting ribbing. Change to C. Beg with a 2nd row, work 2 rows in rib as given for Collar, inc one st at end of 2nd row. Change to B and rib 2 rows, inc one st at end of 2nd row. Change to C and rep last 2 rows. 48 sts. Change to B and rib 1 row. Cast off in rib.
Work right side edge in same way, but inc one st at beg of row.

TO MAKE UP
Join shoulder seams. Sew on sleeves, placing centre of sleeves to shoulder seams. Beg at top of borders, join side seams, then sleeve seams. Mitre corners of collar edgings. Sew on collar and anchor motif. Place ribbon under the collar and tie ends at front.

Trousers

With A, cast on 53 sts. K 7 rows. Beg with a k row, cont in st st until work measures 16cm/6¼in from beg, ending with a p row.
Next row K1, [p1, k1] to end.
Next row P1, [k1, p1] to end.
Rep last 2 rows 3 times more. Cast off in rib.
Make one more piece in same way.
Beginning at ribbed top, join centre back seam and front seam for 13cm/5in, then join leg seams. Join elastic into ring. Place along wrong side of rib and work herring bone casing over it.

Small Teddy with Sweater and Wellingtons

See Page
12

MATERIALS
Teddy Bear 1×50g ball of Rowan Designer DK Wool.
Oddment of Black yarn for embroidery. Stuffing.
Sweater 1×25g hank of Rowan Lightweight DK.
Wellingtons Small amount of Rowan Designer DK Wool.
Pair of 3¼mm (No 10/US 3) knitting needles.

MEASUREMENTS
Teddy Bear Approximately 18cm/7in high.
Sweater Actual chest measurement 14cm/5½in
Length 6cm/2¼in
Sleeve seam 3cm/1¼in

TENSION
28 sts and 36 rows to 10cm/4in square over st st.

ABBREVIATIONS
See page 10.

Teddy Bear

RIGHT LEG
Cast on 10 sts. P 1 row.
Next row K1, [m1, k1] to end. P 1 row.
Next row K7, m1, k1, m1, k8, m1, k1, m1, k2. 23 sts.
Work 3 rows in st st.
Next row K4, [skpo] twice, [k2 tog] twice, k11.
Next row P9, [p2 tog] twice, [p2 tog tbl] twice, p2.
Next row K3, k2 tog, k10. 14 sts.
** Work 3 rows in st st. Inc one st at each end of next row. Work 7 rows.
Next row K1, k2 tog, k1, skpo, k3, k2 tog, k1, skpo, k2. P 1 row.
Next row [K2 tog, k1, skpo, k1] twice.
Next row [P2 tog] to end.
Break off yarn. Thread end through rem sts, pull up and secure. Join sole and inner leg seam, leaving an opening. Stuff firmly and close opening.

LEFT LEG
Cast on 10 sts. P 1 row.
Next row K1, [m1, k1] to end. P 1 row.
Next row K2, m1, k1, m1, k8, m1, k1, m1, k7. 23 sts.
Work 3 rows in st st.
Next row K11, [skpo] twice, [k2 tog] twice, k4.

Next row P2, [p2 tog] twice, [p2 tog tbl] twice, p9.
Next row K10, skpo, k3. 14 sts.
Complete as given for Right Leg from ** to end.

BODY
Begin at neck edge.
Cast on 15 sts. P 1 row.
Next row K1, [m1, k1] to end. 29 sts.
Beg with a p row, work 5 rows in st st.
Next row [K7, m1] twice, k1, [m1, k7] twice.
Work 3 rows.
Next row K16, m1, k1, m1, k16. 35 sts.
Work 5 rows.
Next row K15, skpo, k1, k2 tog, k15.
Work 3 rows.
Next row K14, skpo, k1, k2 tog, k14.
Work 3 rows.
Next row K1, [k2 tog] to end. 16 sts.
P 1 row. Cast off.

ARMS (make 2)
Cast on 6 sts. P 1 row.
Next row K1, [m1, k1] to end. P 1 row.
Next row K1, [m1, k4, m1, k1] twice. 15 sts. Work 3 rows in st st.
Next row K1, [skpo, k2, k2 tog, k1] twice.
Work 3 rows. Inc one st at each end of next row. 13 sts. Work 9 rows.
Next row K1, [skpo, k1, k2 tog, k1] twice. P 1 row.
Next row K1, [k2 tog] to end.
Break off yarn. Thread end through rem sts, pull up and secure. Join underarm seam, leaving an opening. Stuff firmly and close opening.

HEAD
Begin at back. Cast on 7 sts. P 1 row.
Next row K1, [m1, k1] to end.
Rep last 2 rows once more. 25 sts.
Work 3 rows in st st.
Next row K1, [m1, k3] to end. 33 sts.
Work 13 rows.
Next row K1, [k2 tog] to end.
Work 3 rows.
Next row K1, [k2 tog] to end. 9 sts.
P 1 row.
Break off yarn. Thread end through rem sts, pull up and secure. Join seam, leaving an opening. Stuff firmly and close opening.

EARS (make 2)
Cast on 3 sts. P 1 row.
Next row K1, [m1, k1] to end.
Rep last 2 rows once more. 9 sts. P 1 row.
Next row K1, m1, k2, m1, k3, m1, k2, m1, k1. 13 sts.
Work 5 rows in st st.
Next row [K1, skpo] twice, k1, [k2 tog,

k1] twice. P 1 row.
Next row [Skpo] twice, k1, [k2 tog] twice. P 1 row.
Next row Skpo, k1, k2 tog. Cast off.

TO MAKE UP
Fold sides of body to centre, then join cast off edge. Gather neck edge of body, pull up and secure. Join back seam of body, leaving an opening. Stuff firmly and close opening. Sew head in position. Fold ears in half widthwise and stitch together open edge. Sew ears in place. With Black, embroider nose, mouth and eyes. Attach yarn at seam about 1cm/¼in below top of one arm, thread yarn through body at shoulder position, then attach other arm, pull yarn tightly and thread through body again in same place, then attach yarn to first arm again and fasten off. Attach legs at lower edge of body in same way as arms.

Sweater

BACK AND FRONT ALIKE
Cast on 20 sts. Beg with a k row, work 3 rows in st st. Work 3 rows in k2, p2 rib.
Beg with a k row, work 4 rows in st st. Mark each end of last row.
Work a further 3 rows in st st. K 2 rows.
Next row [K1, p1] to end.
Next row [P1, k1] to end.
Rep last 2 rows 3 times.
Shape Shoulders
Cast off 5 sts at beg of next 2 rows. 10 sts. Work 2 rows in k1, p1 rib, inc one st at each end of every row. 14 sts. Rib 1 row. Beg with a k row, work 3 rows in st st. Cast off loosely.

SLEEVES
Join shoulder and neckband seams. With right side facing, pick up and k 20 sts between markers. Work 3 rows in k2, p2 rib. Beg with a k row, work 5 rows in st st. Now work 2 rows in k2, p2 rib. Cast off in rib. Join side and sleeve seams.

Wellingtons

Cast on 10 sts. P 1 row.
Next row K1, [m1, k1] to end. P 1 row.
Next row K1, [m1, k8, m1, k1] twice. 23 sts. Work 3 rows.
Next row K7, [skpo] twice, k1, [k2 tog] twice, k7.
Next row P5, [p2 tog] twice, p1, [p2 tog tbl] twice, p5. 15 sts.
Work 5 rows in st st. K 1 row. Cast off knitwise. Join back seam.
Make one more.

Sailor Doll

See Page
13

MATERIALS
Doll 2×25g hanks of Rowan 4 ply Botany.
Oddments of White, Blue and Red yarn for embroidery.
Pair of 2¾mm (No 12/US 1) knitting needles.
Piece of thin fabric for lining.
Stuffing.
Top, Trousers and Beret 1×25g hanks of Rowan 4 ply Botany in each of Navy (A), Blue (B) and White (C).
Pair each of 2¾mm (No 12/US 1) and 3¼mm (No 10/US 3) knitting needles.
Length of twisted cord and shirring elastic.
Shoes 1×50g ball of Rowan Designer DK Wool.
Pair of 3¼mm (No 10/US 3) knitting needles.
Medium size crochet hook.

MEASUREMENTS
Doll Approximately 41cm/16in high.
Top Actual chest measurement 32cm/12½in
Length 11cm/4¼in
Sleeve seam 9cm/3½in
Trousers Actual hip measurement 30cm/11¾in
Length 20cm/8in
Inside leg seam 10cm/4in

TENSION
34 sts and 46 rows to 10cm/4in square over st st using 4 ply yarn and 2¾mm (No 12/US 1) needles.
28 sts and 40 rows to 10cm/4in square over st st using 4 ply yarn and 3¼mm (No 10/US 3) needles.

ABBREVIATIONS
See page 10.

Doll

BACK
Begin at top of head.
Cast on 43 sts. Beg with a k row, work 44 rows in st st. Mark each end of last row for neck. Work a further 51 rows.
Divide for Legs
Next row P20, cast off next 3 sts, p to end.
Cont on last set of sts for first leg. Work 42 rows in st st. Mark each end of last row. ** Work 6 rows.
Shape Heel
Next row K11, skpo, k1, turn.
Next row P4, p2 tog, p1, turn.
Next row K5, skpo, k1, turn.
Next row P6, p2 tog, p1, turn.
Cont in this way, dec one st as set on every row until 12 sts rem, ending with a p row. Leave these sts on a holder.
With right side facing and beg at marker, pick up and k8 sts from side of heel, k12 sts from holder, pick up and k8 sts from other side of heel to marker. 28 sts. Cont in st st, dec one st at each end of 4 foll 4th rows. 20 sts. Work 7 rows.
Shape Toes
*** **Next row** K1, skpo, k to last 3 sts, k2 tog, k1.
P 1 row. Rep last 2 rows once more. 16 sts. K 1 row.
Next 2 rows P11, turn, k to end.
Next 2 rows P6, turn, k to end. ***
Leave these sts on a spare needle.
With right side facing, rejoin yarn to rem sts for second leg and work as given for first leg, reversing toe shaping.

FRONT
Work as given for Back to **. Work a further 22 rows in st st.
Shape Toes
Work as given for Back from *** to ***.
With right sides of Back and Front together and taking one st from each needle and working them tog, cast off toe sts.
With right side facing, rejoin yarn to rem sts for second leg and complete as given for first leg, reversing toe shaping.

ARMS (make 2)
Cast on 30 sts. Beg with a k row, work 38 rows in st st.
Shape Thumb
Next row K15, m1, k15.
P 1 row.
Next row K15, m1, k1, m1, k15.
P 1 row.
Next row K15, m1, k3, m1, k15.
P 1 row.
Next row K15, m1, k5, m1, k15.
P 1 row.
Next row K22, turn and cast on 1 st.
Next row P8, turn and cast on 1 st.
Work 4 rows on these 9 sts.
Next row K1, [k2 tog] to end.
Break off yarn, thread end through rem sts, pull up, secure, then join thumb seam.
With right side facing, rejoin yarn at base of thumb, pick up and k2 sts from base of thumb, k to end. 32 sts. Work 9 rows.
Shape Fingers
Next 2 rows Work to last 4 sts, turn.
Next 2 rows Work to last 8 sts, turn.
Next 2 rows Work to last 12 sts, turn.
Next row K4.
Fold arm in half with right side to inside and taking one st from each needle and working them tog, cast off.

OUTER LEFT EAR AND INNER RIGHT EAR
Cast on 10 sts. P 1 row.
Next row K1, m1, k to last st, m1, k1.
P 1 row. Rep last 2 rows once more.

Next row K1, m1, k13.
Next row P14, m1, p1.
Next row K1, m1, k15.
Next row P1, p2 tog, p14.
Next row K13, k2 tog, k1.
Next row P1, p2 tog, p12.
Cast off.

OUTER RIGHT EAR AND INNER LEFT EAR
Cast on 10 sts. P1 row.
Next row K1, m1, k to last st, m1, k1.
P1 row. Rep last 2 rows once more.
Next row K13, m1, k1.
Next row P1, m1, p14.
Next row K15, m1, k1.
Next row P14, p2 tog tbl, p1.
Next row K1, skpo, k13.
Next row P12, p2 tog tbl, p1. Cast off.

TO MAKE UP
Join back and front together, leaving cast on edge free. Stuff firmly to neck edge.
Cut 2 circles out of lining approximately 13cm/5in in diameter. Join together, leaving an opening. Stuff firmly and close opening. Insert in head part of body.
Wind length of yarn round neck edge twice, pull up tightly and secure. Place more stuffing between lining and top at front of head to form chin, cheeks and nose. Gather top, pull up and secure.
Divide ends of feet into toes with few straight stitches. Join arm seams, leaving top open. Stuff firmly and close opening.
Divide end of hands into fingers with few straight stitches. With right sides of paired ear pieces together, join seam around, leaving cast on edge free. Turn to right side and stuff slightly. Close opening. Form outline of inner ear with few straight stitches. Sew on arms and ears in place. Embroider eyes with Blue and White yarn. Using Red, embroider mouth. Colour cheeks with red pencil.
Using same yarn as body, make small depressions at centre of cheeks for dimples and at base of nose for nostrils.

Top

BACK
With 3¼mm (No 10/US 3) needles and A, cast on 46 sts. K 3 rows.
Beg with a k row, work in st st for 11cm/4¼in, ending with a p row.
Shape Shoulders
Cast off 6 sts at beg of next 2 rows. Cast off rem 34 sts.

FRONT
Work as given for Back until work measures 6cm/2¼in, ending with a p row.
Shape Neck
Next row K23, turn.
Work on this set of sts only. Dec one st at neck edge on every row until 6 sts rem.

Work few rows straight until Front measures same as Back to cast off edge, ending at side edge. Cast off.
With right side facing, rejoin yarn to rem sts and k to end. Complete as given for first side.

SLEEVES
With 3¼mm (No 10/US 3) needles and A, cast on 30 sts. K 3 rows.
Beg with a k row, work in st st for 9cm/3½in, ending with a p row.
Cast off.

COLLAR
With 3¼ mm (No 10/US 3) needles and B, cast on 46 sts. K 3 rows.
Beg with a k row, work in st st for 5cm/2in, ending with a p row.
Shape Neck
Next row K6, cast off next 34 sts, k to end.
Work on last set of sts only. P1 row.
Next row K twice in first st, k2, k2 tog, k1.
Rep last 2 rows 10 times more. P 1 row.
Next row K3, k2 tog, k1.
P 1 row.
Next row K2, k2 tog, k1.
P 1 row.
Next row K1, k2 tog, k1.
P 1 row.
Next row K2 tog, k1.
P 1 row. K2 tog and fasten off.
With wrong side facing, rejoin yarn to rem sts and p to end.
Next row K1, skpo, k2, k twice in last st.
P 1 row. Rep last 2 rows 10 times more.
Next row K1, skpo, k3.
P 1 row.
Next row K1, skpo, k2.
P 1 row.
Next row K1, skpo, k1.
P 1 row.
Next row K1, skpo.
P 1 row. K2 tog and fasten off.

INSET
With 3¼mm (No 10/US 3) needles and C, cast on 34 sts. K 3 rows.
Beg with a k row, work in st st, dec one st at each end of every row until 2 sts rem.
Cast off.

"TIE"
With 3¼mm (No 10/US 3) needles and A, cast on 5 sts. K 44 rows. Cast off.

TO MAKE UP
Join shoulder seams. Sew on sleeves, placing centre of sleeve tops to shoulder seams. Join side and sleeve seams. With C, swiss darn a "line" around collar. Sew collar in place, then join together pointed ends. Fold "tie" in half widthwise and attach folded end to pointed end of collar. Sew in inset. Place cord under collar and tie ends together at front.

Trousers

FRONT
With 3¼mm (No 10/US 3) needles and A, cast on 30 sts for first side. K 3 rows.
Beg with a k row, work in st st, dec one st at each end of 3rd row and 2 foll 6th rows. 24 sts. Cont straight until work measures 10cm/4in from beg, ending with a p row.
Shape Crotch
Cast off 2 sts at beg of next row. Cont straight until work measures 19cm/7½in from beg, ending with a p row. Work 4 rows in k1, p1 rib. Cast off in rib.
Work second side as given for first side, reversing crotch shaping.

BACK
Work as given for Front.

TO MAKE UP
Join side seams and inside leg seams to crotch shaping. Join centre front and centre back seams. Thread shirring elastic along wrong side of rib, pull up to fit waist of doll and tie ends together.

Beret

With 2¾mm (No 12/US 1) needles and A, cast on 80 sts. K 13 rows.
Change to 3¼mm (No 10/US 3) needles and C.
Next row K4, [m1, k4] to end.
Beg with a p row, work 3 rows in st st.
Next row K4, [m1, k5] to end. 118 sts.

Work 5 rows straight.
Next row K1, [k2 tog tbl, k7] to end.
Work 3 rows.
Next row K1, [k2 tog tbl, k6] to end.
Work 3 rows.
Next row K1, [k2 tog tbl, k5] to end.
Cont in this way, dec 13 sts as set on 3 foll 4th rows, then on foll alt row.
27 sts. P 1 row.
Next row K1, [k2 tog tbl] to end.
Break off yarn, thread end through rem sts, pull up and secure. Join seam.
With 2¾mm (No 12/US 1) needles and A, cast on 5 sts for "tie". K 28 rows. Cast off. Fold "tie" in half widthwise and attach folded edge to base of beret. Place beret on doll's head and secure in position. Form sailor hat with few tuck stitches.

Shoes

SOLE
Cast on 8 sts. Work in st st, inc one st at each end of every alt row until there are 18 sts. Work 10 rows straight. Dec one st at each end of every row until 10 sts rem. Cast off.

UPPER
Cast on 52 sts. K 8 rows.
Next 2 rows K to last 21 sts, turn.
Next 2 rows K to last 22 sts, turn.
Next 2 rows K to last 23 sts, turn.
Next 2 rows K to last 24 sts, turn.
Next row K to end.
Next row K26, turn.
Work on this set of sts only. K 1 row.
Next row K to last 2 sts, k2 tog.
Rep last 2 rows until 19 sts rem. Cast off.
Rejoin yarn at inside edge to rem sts and k to end. K 1 row.
Next row K2 tog, k to end.
Rep last 2 rows until 19 sts rem. Cast off.

TO MAKE UP
Join back seam of upper. Sew in sole. With length of yarn, lace front opening. Make a crochet chain cord approximately 13cm/5in long. Attach centre of cord to top of front opening and tie it into a bow. Make one more.

Pirate Rat

See Page
14

MATERIALS
1×25g hank of Rowan Lightweight DK in each of Grey (A) and Red (B). Small amount of same in each of Black (C), Light Pink (D), Brown (E) and Yellow (F).
Small amount of Rowan 4 ply Botany in each of White (G), Black (H) and Blue (J).
Pair each of 2¾mm (No 12/US 1), 3mm (No 11/US 2) and 3¼mm (No 10/US 3) knitting needles. Medium size crochet hook. Stuffing. Small piece of cardboard and glue.

MEASUREMENTS
Rat Approximately 18cm/7in high.
Shirt Actual chest measurement 15cm/6in
Length 3cm/1¼in
Sleeve seam 2.5cm/1in
Trousers Actual hip measurement 13cm/5in
Length 6cm/2¼in
Inside leg seam 2.5cm/1in

TENSION
30 sts and 38 rows to 10cm/4in square over st st using DK yarn and 3mm (No 11/US 2) needles.

ABBREVIATIONS
See page 10.

Rat

LEGS (make 2)
With 3mm (No 11/US 2) needles and A, cast on 5 sts. P 1 row.
Next row [K twice in next st] to end. 10 sts. Beg with a p row, work 17 rows in st st.
Next row K1, [k2 tog, k1] to end. P 1 row.
Next row P1, [p2 tog] to end.
Break off yarn. Thread end through rem sts, pull up and secure.
Join seam, stuffing as you sew.

BODY
Begin at neck edge. With 3mm (No 11/US 2) needles and A, cast on 9 sts. P 1 row.
Next row [K twice in next st] 4 times, k three times in next st, [k twice in next st] 4 times. 19 sts. P 1 row.
Next row K5, m1, k1, m1, k8, m1, k1, m1, k4. P 1 row.
Next row K6, m1, k1, m1, [k5, m1] twice, k1, m1, k5. P 1 row.
Next row K14, m1, k1, m1, k13. 30 sts. Work 9 rows in st st.
Next row K5, k2 tog, k1, skpo, k3, skpo,

k1, k2 tog, k3, k2 tog, k1, skpo, k4. P 1 row.
Next row K4, k2 tog, k1, skpo, k2, skpo, k3, k2 tog, k1, skpo, k3. P 1 row.
Next row K3, k2 tog, k1, skpo, k4, k2 tog, k1, skpo, k2. 15 sts. P 1 row.
Cast off.
Join back seam, then cast off edge. Stuff. Gather neck edge, pull up and secure.

ARMS (make 2)
With 3mm (No 11/US 2) needles and A, cast on 4 sts. P 1 row.
Next row K1, [m1, k1] to end. 7 sts. Beg with a p row, work 15 rows in st st.
Next row K1, [k2 tog] to end.
Break off yarn. Thread end through rem sts, pull up and secure.
Join seam, stuffing as you sew.

HEAD
With 3mm (No 11/US 2) needles and A, cast on 4 sts. P 1 row.
Next row K1, [m1, k1] to end. P 1 row.
Next row K1, [m1, k2, m1, k1] twice. Work 3 rows in st st.
Next row K1, [m1, k3] 3 times, m1, k1. P 1 row.
Next row K1, m1, k to last st, m1, k1.
Next row P1, m1, p to last st, m1, p1.
Next row K1, [m1, k3] twice, m1, k5, [m1, k3] twice, m1, k1. 25 sts.
Mark each end of last row. Work 6 rows.
Next row P4, p2 tog, p13, p2 tog tbl, p4.
Next row K14, skpo, turn.
Next row Sl 1, p5, p2 tog, turn.
Next row Sl 1, k5, skpo, turn.
Rep last 2 rows 6 times more. Cast off purlwise, working last 2 sts tog.
Join seam from point to markers and stuff head.

OUTER EARS (make 2)
With 3mm (No 11/US 2) needles and A, cast on 7 sts. Beg with a k row, work 4 rows in st st.
Next row Skpo, k3, k2 tog. P 1 row.
Next row Skpo, k1, k2 tog.
P3 tog and fasten off.

INNER EARS (make 2)
With 3mm (No 11/US 2) needles and D, cast on 6 sts. Beg with a k row, work 3 rows in st st.
Next row P2 tog, p2, p2 tog tbl.
Next row Skpo, k2 tog.
P2 tog and fasten off.

TAIL
With 3mm (No 11/US 2) needles and A, cast on 25 sts. Cast off.

TO MAKE UP
Sew head to body. Attach yarn at seam just below top of one arm, thread through body at shoulder position, then attach other arm, pull up yarn tightly and thread through body again in same place,

attach yarn to first arm again and fasten off. Attach legs at lower edge of body in same way as arms. With right sides of inner and outer ears together, join seam all round, leaving cast on edge free. Turn to right side and close opening. Fold this edge in half and secure, then sew in place. With C, embroider face features and whiskers. Attach tail.

Shirt

BACK AND FRONT
With 3mm (No 11/US 2) needles and G, cast on 22 sts. K 3 rows. Beg with a k row, work in st st and stripe patt of 4 rows G and 2 rows H throughout, work 13 rows.
Shape Neck
Next row P7, cast off next 8 sts, p to end.
Next row K7, cast on 8 sts, k to end.
Work a further 13 rows. With G, p 2 rows.
Cast off purlwise.

SLEEVES
With 3mm (No 11/US 2) needles, right side facing and G, pick up and k14 sts between first and last H stripe. Beg with a p row, work 3 rows in st st in G, 2 rows in H and 4 rows in G. With G, p 2 rows.
Cast off purlwise.

TO MAKE UP
Join side and sleeve seams.

Trousers

BACK AND FRONT ALIKE
With 3¼mm (No 10/US 3) needles and B, cast on 18 sts. K 3 rows.
Beg with a k row, work 14 rows in st st.
Next row K7, k2 tog, turn.
Work 3 rows on this set of sts only. K 3 rows. Cast off.
With right side facing, rejoin yarn to rem sts, k2 tog, k to end. Work 3 rows. K 3 rows. Cast off.

BELT
With 3¼mm (No 10/US 3) needles and E, cast on 40 sts. K 3 rows. Cast off.

BUCKLE
With 3¼mm (No 10/US 3) needles and F, cast on 7 sts. K 1 row.
Next row K2, cast off 3, k1 st more.
Next row K2, cast on 3, k2.
K 1 row. Rep last 3 rows once more. Cast off.

TO MAKE UP
Beginning at top of lower garter st borders, join side seams. Join inside leg seam. When on, pull tail through stitches. Attach buckle to one end of belt. Place

belt over trousers below garter st band. Insert other end through buckle and pull up. Attach belt to back of trousers.

Waistcoat

With 3¼mm (No 10/US 3) needles and C, cast on 22 sts. K 15 rows.
Divide for Armholes
Next row K5, cast off next 2 sts, k to last 7 sts, cast off 2 sts, k to end.
Work on last set of sts only for Left Front.
Next row K2 tog, k3. K 5 rows.
Next row K2 tog, k2. K 4 rows. Cast off.
Rejoin yarn to centre sts for Back. K 11 rows. Cast off.
Rejoin yarn to rem sts for Right Front.
Next row K3, k2 tog. K 5 rows.
Next row K2, k2 tog. K 4 rows. Cast off.
Join shoulder seams.

Scarf

With 3¼mm (No 10/US 3) needles and J, cast on 36 sts. K 1 row.

Next 2 rows Cast off 4, k to end.
Beg with a k row, work in st st, dec one st at each end of every row until 2 sts rem.
Work 2 tog and fasten off.

Boots

SOLE
With 2¾mm (No 12/US 1) needles and C, cast on 3 sts. P 1 row.
Next row K1, [m1, k1] twice.
Next row P1, m1, p3, m1, p1. 7 sts.
Beg with a k row, work 4 rows in st st.
Next row Skpo, k3, k2 tog. P 1 row.
Next row Skpo, k1, k2 tog.
P3 tog and fasten off.

UPPER
With 2¾mm (No 12/US 1) needles and C, cast on 24 sts. K 2 rows.
Next row Skpo, k to last 2 sts, k2 tog.
Rep last row 5 times more. 12 sts. K 2 rows.
Next row K1, m1, k to last st, m1, k1.
Rep last row 4 times. 22 sts. Cast off.

TO MAKE UP
Glue soles to piece of cardboard. When dry, cut out soles. Sew cast off edge of uppers to soles, then join front seams, leaving top 9 rows free. With E, lace boots.

Eye Patch

With 3¼mm (No 10/US 3) needles and C, cast on 4 sts. K 4 rows. Cast off.
With crochet hook and C, make a chain, approximately 13cm/5in long. Attach patch to chain. Place in position and tie at back. Secure in place.

Earring

With crochet hook and F, make 4 chains. Attach to ear forming ring.

Small Rabbit with Sweater

See Page 15

MATERIALS
Rabbit 1 × 50g ball of Rowan Designer DK Wool.
Oddment of Black for embroidery.
Stuffing.
Pair of 3¼mm (No 10/US 3) knitting needles.
Sweater 1 × 100g hank of Rowan Magpie Tweed or DK yarn used double.
Pair of 6½mm (No 3/US 10) knitting needles.

MEASUREMENTS
Rabbit Approximately 18cm/7in high.

Sweater Actual chest measurement 19cm/7½in
Length 7cm/2¾in
Sleeve seam 3cm/1¼in

TENSION
28 sts and 36 rows to 10cm/4in square over st st using DK yarn.
15 sts and 23 rows to 10cm/4in square over st st using chunky yarn.

ABBREVIATIONS
See page 10.

Rabbit

LEGS (make 2)
Cast on 12 sts. P 1 row.
Next row K1, [m1, k1] to end. P.1 row.
Next row K1, m1, k8, [m1, k1] 6 times, k7, m1, k1. 31 sts.
Work 3 rows in st st.
Next row K13, k2 tog, k1, skpo, k13. P 1 row.
Next row K12, k2 tog, k1, skpo, k12. 27 sts. P 1 row.
Next row K7, cast off next 13 sts, k to end.
Work 9 rows in st st across all sts, inc one st at each end of 2nd row. 16 sts.

Next row K1, k2 tog, k1, skpo, k3, k2 tog, k1, skpo, k2. P1 row.
Next row K2 tog, k1, skpo, k1, k2 tog, k1, skpo, k1.
Next row [P2 tog] to end.
Break off yarn, thread end through rem sts, pull up and secure. Join instep, sole and back leg seams leaving an opening. Stuff and close opening.

BODY
Begin at neck edge.
Cast on 15 sts. P 1 row.
Next row K1, [m1, k1] to end. 29 sts.
Beg with a p row, work 5 rows in st st.
Next row [K7, m1] twice, k1, [m1, k7] twice.
Work 3 rows.
Next row K16, m1, k1, m1, k16. 35 sts.
Work 5 rows.
Next row K15, skpo, k1, k2 tog, k15.
Work 3 rows.
Next row K14, skpo, k1, k2 tog, k14.
Work 3 rows.
Next row K1, [k2 tog] to end. 16 sts.
P 1 row. Cast off.

ARMS (make 2)
Cast on 6 sts. P 1 row.
Next row K1, [m1, k1] to end. P 1 row.
Next row K1, [m1, k4, m1, k1] twice. 15 sts. Work 7 rows.
Next row K1, [skpo, k2, k2 tog, k1] twice. Work 3 rows. Inc one st at each end of next row. 13 sts. Work 9 rows.
Next row K1, [skpo, k1, k2 tog, k1] twice. P 1 row.
Next row K1, [k2 tog] to end.
Break off yarn, thread end through rem sts, pull up and secure. Join underarm seam, leaving an opening. Stuff firmly and close opening.

HEAD
Begin at back.
Cast on 7 sts. P1 row.
Next row K1, [m1, k1] to end.
Rep last 2 rows once more. 25 sts.
Work 3 rows in st st.
Next row K1, [m1, k3] to end. 33 sts.
Work 13 rows.
Next row K1, [k2, tog] to end.
Work 5 rows.

Next row K1, [k2 tog] to end. 9 sts.
P1 row.
Break off yarn, thread end through rem sts, pull up and secure. Join seam, leaving an opening. Stuff firmly and close opening.

EARS (make 2)
Cast on 14 sts. K 30 rows.
Next row Skpo, k to last 2 sts, k2 tog.
K 1 row.
Rep last 2 rows until 2 sts rem. K2 tog and fasten off.

TO MAKE UP
Fold sides of body to centre, then join cast off edge. Gather neck edge of body, pull up and secure. Join back seam, leaving an opening. Stuff firmly and close opening. Sew head in position. Fold cast on edge of ears, making top folds smaller, sew them in place. With Black, embroider nose, mouth and eyes. Attach yarn at seam about 1cm/¼in below top of one arm, thread yarn through body at shoulder position, then attach other arm, pull yarn tightly and thread through body again in same place, then attach yarn to first arm again and fasten off. Attach legs at lower edge of body in same way as arms.

Sweater

BACK AND FRONT ALIKE
Cast on 14 sts. Work 2 rows in k1, p1 rib.
Beg with a k row, work 5 rows in st st.
Mark each end of last row. Work a further 7 rows.
Shape Shoulders
Next row Cast off 3 sts (1 st on needle), p1, [k1, p1] 3 times, cast off rem 3 sts.
With wrong side facing, rejoin yarn to rem 8 sts, work twice in first st, rib to last st, work twice in last st. Rib 3 rows more, inc one st at each end of first row. 12 sts.
Cast off in rib.

SLEEVES
Join shoulder and neckband seams. With right side facing, pick up and k14 sts between markers. Beg with a p row, work 3 rows in st st. Work 2 rows in k1, p1 rib.
Cast off in rib.
Join side and sleeve seams.

Farm Play Mat

See Page
16

MATERIALS
Play mat 1×50g ball of Rowan Designer DK Wool in each of Light Green, Bright Green, Dark Green, Khaki, Gold, Light Brown, Mid Brown, Dark Brown, Light Grey and Dark Grey.
Pair each of 4mm (No 8/US 5) and 3¼mm (No 10/US 3) knitting needles.
Cable needle.
Piece of 38cm×48cm/15in×19in Green felt.
Stuffing.
Animals 1×50g ball of Rowan Designer DK Wool in each of Mid Brown, Cream, Black and Pink.
Small amount of same in each of Beige and Light Brown.
Oddment of 4 ply yarn in Gold.
Pair of 3¼mm (No 10/US 3) knitting needles.
Crochet hook.
Stuffing.

MEASUREMENTS
Play mat Approximately 38cm×48cm/ 15in×19in.
Bull Approximately 8cm/3in high and 13cm/5in long.
Cow Approximately 7cm/2¾in high and 11cm/4¼in long.
Sheep Approximately 5cm/2in high and 8cm/3in long.
Pig Approximately 5cm/2in high and 8cm/3in long.
Piglet Approximately 1.5cm/½in high and 3cm/1¼in long.

TENSION
24 sts and 32 rows to 10cm/4in square over st st on 4mm (No 8/US 5) needles.
26 sts and 50 rows to 10cm/4in square over garter st (every row k) on 3¼mm (No 10/US 3) needles.
28 sts and 36 rows to 10cm/4in square over st st on 3¼mm (No 10/US 3) needles.

ABBREVIATIONS
C6B=slip next 3 sts onto cable needle and leave at back of work, [k1 tbl] 3 times, then k3 from cable needle. Also see page 10.

Play Mat

SQUARE A (make 2)
With 4mm (No 8/US 5) needles and Light Brown, cast on 29 sts. K 1 row.
1st row K4, [p1, k1] to last 3 sts, k3.
Rep this row 39 times more. K 2 rows.
Cast off.

SQUARE B (make 2)
With 4mm (No 8/US 5) needles and Bright Green, cast on 31 sts. K 3 rows.
1st row (right side) K.
2nd row K2, p27, k2.
Rep last 2 rows 17 times more. K 3 rows.
Cast off.

SQUARE C
With 4mm (No 8/US 5) needles and Khaki, cast on 29 sts. K 3 rows.
1st row K4, [p1, k1] to last 3 sts, k3.
Rep last row 45 times more. K 3 rows.
Cast off.

SQUARE D (make 2)
With 4mm (No 8/US 5) needles and Gold, cast on 38 sts. K 1 row.
1st row (right side) K3, p7, * k3, [k1 tbl] 3 times, p6; rep from * once more, p1, k3.
2nd row K10, * [p1 tbl] 3 times, p3, k6; rep from * once more, k4.
3rd and 4th rows As 1st and 2nd rows.
5th row K3, p7, [C6B, p6] twice, p1, k3.
6th row As 2nd row.
7th row K3, p1, k3, [k1 tbl] 3 times, *p6, k3, [k1 tbl] 3 times; rep from * once more, p1, k3.
8th row K4, [p1 tbl] 3 times, p3, * k6, [p1 tbl] 3 times, p3; rep from * once more, k4.
9th and 10th rows As 7th and 8th rows.
11th row K3, p1, C6B, [p6, C6B] twice, p1, k3.
12th row As 8th row.
Rep these 12 rows twice more, then work 1st to 6th rows again. K 2 rows.
Cast off.

SQUARE E (make 2)
With 4mm (No 8/US 5) needles and Mid Brown, cast on 28 sts. K 1 row.
1st row (right side) K3, [k into the back of 2nd st, k first st, slip both sts off needle tog, k2] 6 times, k1.
2nd row K3, [p into the front of 2nd st, p first st, slip both sts off needle tog, k2] 6 times, k1.
Rep last 2 rows 22 times more. K 2 rows.
Cast off.

SQUARE F
With Light Green, work as given for Square C.

SQUARE G
With 4mm (No 8/US 5) needles and Khaki, cast on 31 sts. K 3 rows.
1st row (right side) K.
2nd row K2, p27, k2.
Rep last 2 rows 16 times more. K 3 rows.
Cast off.

SQUARE H
With Light Green, work as given for Square G.

STRAW BALES (make 5)

With 3¼mm (No 10/US 3) needles and Gold, cast on 8 sts. Work 12 rows in st st. Cast off. Join cast on and cast off edges together and stuff.

With 3¼mm (No 10/US 3) needles and Gold, cast on 3 sts. K 1 row.
Next row K1, k twice in next st, k1.
Next row K2, k twice in next st, k1.
Next row K2, k2 tog, k1.
Next row K1, k2 tog, k1.
K3 tog and fasten off. Make one more. Sew sides to each end of bale.

FENCES (make 3)

With 3¼mm (No 10/US 3) needles and Dark Brown, cast on 30 sts for cross bar. K 1 row. Cast off.
With 3¼mm (No 10/US 3) needles and Dark Brown, cast on 8 sts for large post. Work 5 rows in st st. Cast off. Make 3 more.
With 3¼mm (No 10/US 3) needles and Dark Brown, cast on 5 sts for small post. Work 5 rows in st st. Cast off.
Join cast on and cast off edges of posts together and close openings at each end. Sew posts to cross bar, with smaller post at one end.

HEDGES (make 4)

With 3¼mm (No 10/US 3) needles and Dark Green, cast on 22 sts.
1st row (right side) P.
2nd row K1, *[k1, p1, k1] all in next st, p3 tog; rep from * to last st, k1.
3rd row P.
4th row K1, * p3 tog, [k1, p1, k1] all in next st; rep from * to last st, k1.
Rep last 4 rows 3 times more. P 1 row. Cast off.
Fold in half and catch together cast on and cast off edges at each end.

WALLS (make 3)

With 3¼mm (No 10/US 3) needles and Dark Grey, cast on 23 sts.
1st and 2nd rows With Dark Grey, k.
3rd row With Light Grey, k1, sl 1, [k3, sl 1] 5 times, k1.
4th row With Light Grey, p1, sl 1, [p3, sl 1] 5 times, p1.
5th and 6th rows As 1st and 2nd rows.
7th row With Light Grey, k3, [sl 1, k3] to end.
8th row With Light Grey, p3, [sl 1, p3] to end.
Work 1st to 6th rows again. With Dark Grey, cast off.
Make one more. Join two pieces together stuffing slightly. Fold wall at centre to form corner and catch top and bottom at folded end.

TO MAKE UP

Beginning at lower right corner, join squares in rows of 3 in following order: A, B, C, D, E, F, G, B, D, A, H and E. Place piece of felt under patchwork. Pad slightly squares B, C and F. Sew patchwork to felt. Sew down individual squares, paying special attention to padded squares. Place "field" features on mat as desired.

Bull

BODY AND HEAD

With 3¼mm (No 10/US 3) needles and Mid Brown, cast on 28 sts. K 32 rows.
Next row K2 tog tbl, k5, k2 tog, k10, k2 tog tbl, k5, k2 tog.
K 1 row.
Next row K2 tog tbl, k to last 2 sts, k2 tog.
Rep last 2 rows twice more. 18 sts. K 2 rows.
Shape Head
Next 2 rows K to last 5 sts, turn.
Next 2 rows K to last 6 sts, turn.
Next 2 rows K to last 7 sts , turn.
Next row K to end.
Next row K2 tog, k to last 2 sts, k2 tog. 16 sts. K 9 rows.
Next row [K2 tog] to end.
Break off yarn, thread end through rem sts, pull and secure.

LEGS (make 4)

With 3¼mm (No 10/US 3) needles and Mid Brown, cast on 8 sts. K 10 rows. Cast off.

EARS (make 2))

With 3¼mm (No 10/US 3) needles and Mid Brown, cast on 5 sts. K 2 rows.
Next row K2 tog, k1, k2 tog.
K1 row. K3 tog and fasten off.

HORNS

With 3¼mm (No 10/US 3) needles and Beige, cast on 14 sts. Cast off.

TAIL

With 3¼mm (No 10/US 3) needles and Mid Brown, cast on 16 sts. Cast off.

TO MAKE UP

Fold body and head in half lengthwise and join underside seam, leaving cast on edge free. Stuff and close opening. Join cast on and cast off edges of legs and one row ends edge. Stuff legs and sew open ends to body. Make a small tassel in Mid Brown and attach to one end of tail, sew other end in place. Sew on ears.** Place centre of horns on top of head between ears and over sew in position with Mid Brown yarn. With crochet hook and Gold yarn, make chain approximately 2cm/¾in long. Attach to nose forming ring. Embroider eyes with Beige.

Cow

BODY AND HEAD

With 3¼mm (No 10/US 3) needles and Cream, cast on 28 sts. K 32 rows.
Next row K2 tog tbl, k5, k2 tog, k10, k2 tog tbl, k5, k2 tog.
K 1 row.
Next row K2 tog tbl, k to last 2 sts, k2 tog.
Rep last 2 rows 3 times more. 16 sts.
Shape Head
Next 2 rows K to last 5 sts, turn.
Next 2 rows K to last 6 sts, turn.

Next 2 rows K to last 7 sts, turn.
Next row K to end.
Next row K2 tog, k to last 2 sts, k2 tog. 14 sts. K 9 rows.
Next row [K2 tog] to end.
Break off yarn, thread end through rem sts, pull up and secure.

LEGS (make 4)

With 3¼mm (No 10/US 3) needles and Cream, cast on 6 sts. K 10 rows. Cast off.

SPOTS

With 3¼mm (No 10/US 3) needles and Mid Brown, cast on 5 sts. Work in garter st, inc one st at each end of 2 foll alt rows. 9 sts. K 7 rows. Dec one st at each end of next row and foll alt row. K 1 row. Cast off.
With 3¼mm (No 10/US 3) needles and Mid Brown, cast on 5 sts. Work in garter st, inc one st at each end of 2 foll alt rows. 9 sts. K 5 rows. Dec one st at each end of next row and foll alt row. Cast off.
With 3¼mm (No 10/US 3) needles and Mid Brown, cast on 3 sts. Work in garter st, inc one st at each end of 2 foll alt rows. 7 sts. K2 rows. Dec one st at each end of next row and foll alt row. Cast off.

EARS (make 2)

With 3¼mm (No 10/US 3) needles and Cream, cast on 5 sts. Work in garter st, dec one st at each end of 3rd row. K 1 row. K 3 tog and fasten off.

HORNS

With 3¼mm (No 10/US 3) needles and Light Brown, cast on 10 sts. Cast off.

TAIL

With 3¼mm (No 10/US 3) needles and Cream, cast on 16 sts. Cast off.

TO MAKE UP

Work as given for To Make Up of Bull to ** using Cream for tassel. Place centre of horns on top of head between ears and over sew in position with Cream yarn. Sew on spots. Embroider eyes and nostrils with Mid Brown.

Sheep

BODY AND HEAD

With 3¼mm (No 10/US 3) needles and Cream, cast on 20 sts. K 18 rows.
Next row K2 tog, k to last 2 sts, k2 tog.
K 1 row.
Rep last 2 rows twice more.
Change to Black. Beg with a k row, work 8 rows in st st. Break off yarn, thread end through sts, pull up and secure.

LEGS (make 4)

With 3¼mm (No 10/US 3) needles and Black, cast on 7 sts. Work 5 rows in st st. Break off yarn, thread end through sts, pull up and join seam, stuffing as you sew.

EARS (make 2)

With 3¼mm (No 10/US 3) needles and Black, cast on 5 sts. K 2 rows.

Next row K2 tog, k1, k2 tog.
K1 row. K3 tog and fasten off.

TAIL
With 3¼mm (No 10/US 3) needles and
Black, cast on 4 sts. Work 4 rows in st st.
Cast off.

TO MAKE UP
Fold body and head in half lengthwise
and join underside seam, leaving cast on
edge free. Stuff and close opening. Sew
on legs and ears. Fold tail in half lengthwise and join seam. Sew tail in place.
Embroider eyes with Cream.
Work 1 more sheep for standing sheep
and 2 more omitting legs for lying down
sheep.

Pigs

BODY AND HEAD
With 3¼mm (No 10/US 3) needles and
Pink, cast on 22 sts. Beg with a k row,
work 16 rows in st st.
Shape Head
Next row K8, k2 tog, k2, skpo, k8.

P 1 row.
Next row K7, k2 tog, k2, skpo, k7.
P 1 row.
Next row K6, k2 tog, k2, skpo, k6.
P 1 row.
Next row K5, k2 tog, k2, skpo, k5.
P 1 row.
Next row K4, k2 tog, k2, skpo, k4.
K 1 row.
Next row [K2 tog] to end.
Break off yarn, thread end through rem
sts, pull up and secure.

LEGS (make 2)
With 3¼mm (No 10/US 3) needles and
Pink, cast on 5 sts. Work 6 rows in st st.
Break off yarn, thread end through sts,
pull up and join seam, stuffing as you
sew.

EARS (make 2)
With 3¼mm (No 10/US 3) needles and
Pink, cast on 5 sts. K 1 row. P 1 row.
Next row K2 tog tbl, k1, k2 tog.
P 1 row. K3 tog and fasten off.

TAIL
With 3¼mm (No 10/US 3) needles and
Pink, cast on 10 sts. Cast off.

TO MAKE UP
Fold body and head in half lengthwise and
join underside seam, leaving cast on edge
free. Stuff and close opening. Sew on legs
and ears. Thread yarn through width of tail
and pull up slightly, then sew to body.
Embroider eyes and nostrils with Black.
Work 1 more pig omitting legs for lying
down pig. With Pink, embroider row of
"teats".

Piglets

With 3¼mm (No 10/US 3) needles and
Pink, cast on 8 sts. Work 8 rows in st st.
Break off yarn, thread end through sts,
pull up and join seam, stuffing as you
sew. Join cast on edge. With darning
needle and Pink, make chains for tail
and by oversewing, embroider ears.
Make 2 more.

Sheep

See Page
19

Ram

UPPER BODY
With MC, cast on 58 sts. K 1 row. Mark
centre of last row. Cont in garter st.

MATERIALS

Ram 3×50g balls of Rowan Designer
DK Wool in Cream (MC) and 1 ball of
Black (A).
Small amount of same in Brown.
Pair of 3¼mm (No 10/US 3) knitting
needles.
Stuffing.
Ewe 4×25g hanks of Rowan
Lightweight DK in Cream (MC) and 1
hank in Black (A).
Pair of 3mm (No 11/US 2) knitting
needles.
Stuffing.
Lamb 2×25g hanks of Rowan 4 ply
Botany in Cream (MC) and 1 hank in
Black (A).
Pair of 2¾mm (No 12/US 1) knitting
needles.
Stuffing.

MEASUREMENTS

Ram Approximately 23cm/9in high
and 46cm/18in long.
Ewe Approximately 20cm/8in high and
41cm/16in long.
Lamb Approximately 15cm/6in high
and 33cm/13in long.

TENSION
26 sts and 50 rows to 10cm/4in square
over garter st (every row k) using
DK yarn and 3¼mm (No 10/US 3)
needles.
28 sts and 54 rows to 10cm/4in square
over garter st (every row k) using DK
yarn and 3mm (No 11/US 2) needles.
31 sts and 66 rows to 10cm/4in square
over garter st (every row k) using 4 ply
yarn and 2¾mm (No 12/US 1)
needles.

ABBREVIATIONS
See page 10.

Shape Back Legs
Cast on 6 sts at beg of next 4 rows and 3
sts at beg of foll 2 rows. 88 sts.
Work 20 rows straight. Cast off 3 sts at
beg of next 2 rows. Dec one st at each
end of next row, 2 foll alt rows, then on foll

3 rows. 70 sts.
Inc one st at each end of 7th row and 2
foll 6th rows. 76 sts. Work 29 rows. Dec
one st at each end of next row and 2 foll
6th rows. 70sts. Work 7 rows.
Shape Front Legs
Cast on 3 sts at beg of next 6 rows. 88
sts. Work 20 rows. Cast off 3 sts at beg of
next 4 rows. Dec one st at each end of
next row and 5 foll alt rows, then on every
row until 38 sts rem. Work 3 rows. Cast
off.

UNDERSIDE
With MC, cast on 5 sts. Mark centre st.
Work in garter st, inc one st at each end
of 3rd row, foll alt row and 3 foll 8th rows.
15 sts. Work 9 rows.
Shape Back Legs
Cast on 6 sts at beg of next 4 rows and 3
sts at beg of foll 2 rows. 45 sts. Work 1
row.
Next row K15, k2 tog tbl, k11, k2 tog,
k15.
Work 3 rows.
Next row K14, k2 tog tbl, k11, k2 tog,
k14.
Cont in this way, dec 2 sts as set on
every foll 4th row until 35 sts rem. Work 2
rows. Cast off 3 sts at beg of next row.
Next row Cast off 3 sts, k6 sts more, k2
tog tbl, k11, k2 tog, k to end.
Dec one st at each end of next row and 2
foll alt rows, then on foll 3 rows. 15 sts.
Inc one st at each end of 7th row and 2

foll 6th rows. 21 sts. Work 29 rows. Dec one st at each end of next row and 2 foll 6th rows. 15 sts. Work 7 rows.

Shape Front Legs

Cast on 3 sts at beg of next 6 rows. 33 sts. Work 20 rows. Cast off 3 sts at beg of next 4 rows. Dec one st at each end of next row and every foll 6th row until 9 sts rem. Work 3 rows. Cast off.

HEAD

With A, cast on 47 sts.
Next row K37, turn.
Next row P27, turn.
Next row K23, turn.
Next row P19, turn.
Next row K15, turn.
Next row P11, turn.
Next row K to end.
Beg with a p row, work 5 rows in st st.
Next row K7, k2 tog, k6, k2 tog tbl, k13, k2 tog, k6, k2 tog tbl, k7.
Next row P14, p2 tog, p11, p2 tog tbl, p14.
Next row K6, k2 tog, k6, k2 tog tbl, k9, k2 tog, k6, k2 tog tbl, k6.
Next row P13, p2 tog, p7, p2 tog tbl, p13.
Next row K5, [k2 tog, k6, k2 tog tbl, k5] twice.
P 1 row.
Next row K4, k2 tog, k6, k2 tog tbl, k3, k2 tog, k6, k2 tog tbl, k4.
Work 3 rows.
Next row K10, k2 tog, k3, k2 tog tbl, k10.
Work 9 rows, dec one st at centre of 7th row. 24 sts.

Shape Muzzle

Next row K3, cast off next 6 sts, k5 sts more, cast off next 6 sts, k to end.
Work 3 rows on last set of 3 sts. Leave these sts on a holder.
With wrong side facing, rejoin yarn to centre 6 sts and work 3 rows.
Leave these sts on a holder.
With wrong side facing, rejoin yarn to rem 3 sts and work 3 rows.
Slip these sts and last 3 sts on a holder

onto one needle. Place these sts to centre 6 sts with right sides together, then cast them off together.

FEET (make 8)

With A, cast on 14 sts. Work 14 rows in st st. Cast off.

HORNS (make 2)

With Brown, cast on 12 sts. P 1 row. K 1 row. P 2 rows. These 4 rows form patt. Cont in patt, dec one st at each end of 7th row and every foll 4th row until 2 sts rem, ending with a wrong side row. P2 tog and fasten off.

EARS (make 2)

With A, cast on 6 sts. Work in garter st, dec one st at each end of 5th row and foll alt row. K 1 row. K2 tog and fasten off.

TAIL

With MC, cast on 24 sts. K 2 rows. Cast off.

TO MAKE UP

Join upper body to underside, matching markers and legs and leaving row ends of legs free. Fold first 2 sts of row ends of legs to inside and slip st in place. Join paired feet pieces together, leaving one row end edge open. Place open end of feet inside legs and sew in position. Fold last 3 rows of cast off edge of body and underside to inside and slip st in place. Join head seam. Place cast off seam of muzzle at centre, then join row ends to cast off sts. Stuff body and head. Sew head to body.** Roll horns widthwise and stitch top edge, then pull thread, thus curling the horns. Sew horns, ears and tail in place. With MC, embroider eyes.

Ewe

UPPER BODY, UNDERSIDE, HEAD, FEET, EARS AND TAIL

Work as given for Upper Body, Underside, Head, Feet, Ears and Tail of Ram.

TO MAKE UP

Work as given for To Make Up of Ram to **. Sew ears and tail in place. With MC, embroider eyes.

Lamb

UPPER BODY, UNDERSIDE AND HEAD

Work as given for Upper Body, Underside and Head of Ram.

FEET (make 4)

With A, cast on 10 sts. Work 20 rows in st st. Cast off.

EARS (make 2)

Work as given for Ears of Ram.

TAIL

With MC, cast on 20 sts. K 1 row. Cast off.

TO MAKE UP

Join upper body to underside, matching markers and legs and leaving row ends of legs free. Fold first 2 sts of row ends of legs to inside and slip st in place. Fold feet in half widthwise and join cast on and cast off edges and one row ends edge. Place open edge of feet inside legs and sew in place. Fold last 3 rows of cast off edge of body and underside to inside and slip stitch in place. Join head seam. Place cast off seam of muzzle at centre, then join row ends to cast off sts. Stuff body and head. Sew head to body. Sew ears and tail in place. With MC, embroider eyes.

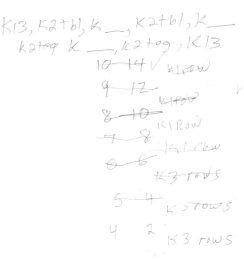

Pig and Piglets

See Page
18

MATERIALS
Pig 3×50g balls of Rowan Designer DK Wool.
Piglet 1×50g ball of Rowan Designer DK Wool.

Oddments of Black yarn for embroidery.
Pair of 3¼mm (No10/US 3) knitting needles. Stuffing.

MEASUREMENTS
Pig Approximately 20cm/8in high and 31cm/12¼in long.
Piglet Approximately 10cm/4in high and 19cm/7½in long.

TENSION
26 sts and 50 rows to 10cm/4in square over garter st (every row k).

ABBREVIATIONS
See page 10.

Pig

UPPER BODY
Cast on 80 sts. Mark centre of cast on edge. Work in garter st throughout, k 1 row.
Shape Back Legs
Cast on 4 sts at beg of next 6 rows and 6 sts at beg of foll 2 rows. 116 sts. K 22 rows. Cast off 6 sts at beg of next 2 rows, then 4 sts at beg of foll 4 rows and 2 sts at beg of foll 4 rows. 80 sts. K 36 rows.
Shape Front Legs
Cast on 3 sts at beg of next 4 rows and 6 sts at beg of foll 4 rows. 116 sts. K 18 rows. Cast off 6 sts at beg of next 6 rows. 80 sts. K 9 rows.
Shape Head
Next row [K13, k2 tog tbl] twice, k20, [k2 tog, k13] twice.
K 3 rows.
Next row K13, k2 tog tbl, k12, k2 tog tbl, k18, k2tog, k12, k2 tog, k13.
K 3 rows.
Next row K13, k2 tog tbl, k11, k2 tog tbl, k16, k2 tog, k11, k2 tog, k13.
Cont in this way, dec 4 sts as set on 4 foll alt rows and 3 foll 4th rows. 40 sts. K 3 rows. Cast off.
Snout
Commencing at beginning of cast off row of Upper Body, pick up and k 40 sts along cast off row. K 9 rows. Cast off.

UNDERSIDE
Cast on 5 sts. Mark centre st. Work in garter st throughout, k 1 row. Inc one st at each end of next 4 rows, then 2 foll alt rows and foll 4th row. 19 sts. K 25 rows. Dec one st at each end of next row and 2

foll alt rows. 13 sts. K 4 rows.
Shape Back Legs
Cast on 4 sts at beg of next row.
Next row Cast on 4 sts, k4, k2 tog tbl, k9, k2 tog, k4.
Cast on 4 sts at beg of next 3 rows.
Next row Cast on 4 sts, k12, k2 tog tbl, k7, k2 tog, k12.
Cast on 6 sts at beg of next 2 rows. K 1 row.
Next row K18, k2 tog tbl, k5, k2 tog, k18.
K 3 rows.
Next row K18, k2 tog tbl, k3, k2 tog, k18.
K 3 rows.
Next row K18, k2 tog tbl, k1, k2 tog, k18.
K 3 rows.
Next row K18, m1, k3, m1, k18.
K 3 rows.
Next row K18, m1, k5, m1, k18.
K 3 rows.
Next row K18, m1, k7, m1, k18.
Cast off 6 sts at beg of next 2 rows and 4 sts at beg of foll row.
Next row Cast off 4 sts, k7 sts more, m1, k9, m1, k8.
Cast off 4 sts at beg of next 2 rows and 2 sts at beg of foll row.
Next row Cast off 2 sts, k1 st more, m1, k11, m1, k2.
Cast off 2 sts at beg of next 2 rows. 13 sts. Inc one st at each end of 2nd row, then foll 4th row and foll 6th row. 19 sts. K 11 rows. Dec one st at each end of next row, then foll 6th row and foll 4th row. K 2 rows.
Shape Front Legs
Cast on 3 sts at beg of next 3 rows.
Next row Cast on 3 sts, k6, k2 tog tbl, k9, k2 tog, k6.
Cast on 6 sts at beg of next 3 rows.
Next row Cast on 6 sts, k18, k2 tog tbl, k7, k2 tog, k18.
K 3 rows.
Next row K18, k2 tog tbl, k5, k2 tog, k18.
K 3 rows.
Next row K18, k2 tog tbl, k3, k2 tog, k18.
K1 row.
Next row K18, m1, k5, m1, k18.
K 3 rows.
Next row K18, m1, k7, m1, k18.
K 3 rows.
Next row K18, m1, k9, m1, k18.
Cast off 6 sts at beg of next 3 rows.
Next row Cast off 6 sts, k 5 sts more, m1, k11, m1, k6.
Cast off 6 sts at beg of next 2 rows. 13 sts. K 8 rows. Dec one st at each end of next row, then 2 foll 6th rows and 2 foll 4th rows. K 1 row. K3 tog and fasten off.

SNOUT CENTRE
Cast on 3 sts. Work in garter st throughout, k 1 row. Inc one st at each end of next 3 rows and 2 foll alt rows. 13 sts.

K 11 rows. Dec one st at each end of next row, then on 2 foll alt rows and foll 2 rows. K 1 row. Cast off.

EARS (make 2)
Cast on 21 sts. Work in garter st throughout, k 10 rows. Dec one st at each end of next row and 3 foll 4th rows, then on every alt row until 3 sts rem. K 1 row. Cast off.

TAIL
Cast on loosely 16 sts. Cast off tightly.

TO MAKE UP
Join snout seam, then sew in snout centre. Join upper body to underside, matching legs and markers and leaving an opening. Stuff firmly and close opening. Make small pleat at centre of cast on edge of ears and sew them in place. Sew on tail. With Black, embroider eyes, nostrils and mouth.

Piglet

UPPER BODY
Cast on 40 sts. Mark centre of cast on row. Work in garter st throughout, k 1 row.
Shape Back Legs
Cast on 3 sts at beg of next 6 rows. 58 sts. K 10 rows. Cast off 3 sts at beg of next 6 rows. 40 sts. K 18 rows.
Shape Front Legs
Cast on 3 sts at beg of next 6 rows. 58 sts. K 8 rows. Cast off 3 sts at beg of next 6 rows. 40 sts. K 4 rows.
Shape Head
Next row K5, k2 tog tbl, k6, k2 tog tbl, k10, k2 tog, k6, k2 tog, k5.
K 3 rows.
Next row [K5, k2 tog tbl] twice, k8, [k2 tog, k5] twice.
K 1 row.
Next row K5, k2 tog tbl, k4, k2 tog tbl, k6, k2 tog, k4, k2 tog, k5.
K 1 row.
Next row K5, k2 tog tbl, k3, k2 tog tbl, k4, k2 tog, k3, k2 tog, k5.
K 3 rows.
Next row K5, [k2 tog tbl, k2] twice, k2 tog, k2, k2 tog, k5.
20 sts. K 2 rows. Cast off.
Snout
Commencing at beginning of cast off row of Upper Body, pick up and k20 sts along cast off row. K 5 rows. Cast off.

UNDERSIDE
Cast on 3 sts. Mark centre st. Work in garter st throughout, k 1 row. Inc one st at each end of next 2 rows, then on foll alt row. 9 sts. K 18 rows. Dec one st at each end of next row. K 4 rows.
Shape Back Legs
Cast on 3 sts at beg of next row.
Next row Cast on 3 sts, k3, k2 tog tbl,

k3, k2 tog, k3.
Cast on 3 sts at beg of next 2 rows.
Next row Cast on 3 sts, k9, k2 tog tbl, k1, k2 tog, k6.
Cast on 3 sts at beg of next row. K 1 row.
Next row K9, sl 1, k2 tog, psso, k9.
K 4 rows.
Next row K9, m1, k1, m1, k9.
K 2 rows.
Next row K9, m1, k3, m1, k9.
Cast off 3 sts at beg of next 2 rows.
Next row Cast off 3 sts, k2 sts more, m1, k5, m1, k6.
Cast off 3 sts at beg of next 3 rows.
K 4 rows. Inc one st at each end of next row. K 9 rows. Dec one st at each end of next row. K 3 rows.
Shape Front Legs
Cast on 3 sts at beg of next row.
Next row Cast on 3 sts, k3, k2 tog tbl, k3, k2 tog, k3.

Cast on 3 sts at beg of next 2 rows.
Next row Cast on 3 sts, k9, k2 tog tbl, k1, k2 tog, k6.
Cast on 3 sts at beg of next row. K 1 row.
Next row K9, sl 1, k2 tog, psso, k9.
K 2 rows.
Next row K9, m1, k1, m1, k9.
K 2 rows.
Next row K9, m1, k3, m1, k9.
Cast off 3 sts at beg of next 2 rows.
Next row Cast off 3 sts, k2 sts more, m1, k5, m1, k6.
Cast off 3 sts at beg of next 3 rows. K 8 rows. Dec one st at each end of next row and foll 4th row. K 3 rows. K3 tog and fasten off.

SNOUT CENTRE
Cast on 2 sts. Work in garter st throughout, k 1 row. Inc one st at each end of next row and foll alt row. 6 sts. K 6 rows.

Dec one st at each end of next row and foll alt row. Cast off.

EARS
Cast on 11 sts. Work in garter st throughout, k 6 rows. Dec one st at each end of next row and foll 4th row, then on 2 foll alt rows. Work 1 row. K 3 tog and fasten off.

TAIL
Cast on loosely 9 sts. Cast off tightly.

TO MAKE UP
Join snout seam, then sew in snout centre. Join upper body to underside, matching legs and markers and leaving an opening. Stuff firmly and close opening. Make small pleat at centre of cast on edge of ears and sew them in place. Sew on tail. With Black, embroider eyes, nostrils and mouth.

Cow and Bull

See Page
20

MATERIALS
Cow 3×50g balls of Rowan Designer DK Wool in Cream (MC) and 1 ball in Rust (A).
Small amount of same in each of Pink, Brown and Black.
Bull 4×50g balls of Rowan Designer DK Wool in Black (MC).
Small amount of same in Brown.
Small metal ring.

Pair of 3¼mm (No 10/US 3) knitting needles.
Stuffing.

MEASUREMENTS
Approximately 23cm/9in high and 41cm/16in long.

TENSION
26 sts and 50 rows to 10cm/4in square over garter st (every row k).

ABBREVIATIONS
See page 10.

NOTE
When working in pattern, use separate small balls of yarn for each coloured area and twist yarns together on wrong side at joins to avoid holes.

Cow

UPPER BODY
Left Back Leg With MC, cast on 20 sts. K 1 row. Cont in garter st, inc one st at beg of next row and at same edge on every row until there are 31 sts. K 1 row. Leave these sts on a holder.

Right Back Leg With MC, cast on 20 sts. K 1 row. Cont in garter st, inc one st at end of next row and at same edge on every row until there are 31 sts. K 1 row.
Shape Body
Next row (right side) K across sts of Right Back Leg, cast on 58 sts, then k across Left Back Leg sts. 120 sts.
Mark centre of last row. K 3 rows. Cast off 13 sts at beg of next 2 rows. Dec one st at each end of next row and 3 foll alt rows. 86 sts. K 1 row.
Place chart 1 as follows
Next row With MC, k2 tog, k14, reading chart 1 from right to left, k across 1st row, k8MC, reading chart 1 from left to right, k across 1st row, with MC, k14, k2 tog.
Next row K15MC, reading chart 1 from right to left, k across 2nd row, k8MC, reading chart 1 from left to right, k across 2nd row, k15MC.
Cont working from chart 1 as set, dec one st at each end of next row and 3 foll alt rows, then at each end of foll 2 rows. 72 sts. Patt 11 rows straight.
Now inc one st at each end of next row and 2 foll alt rows, then on foll 4th row. 80 sts. Patt 1 row.
Place chart 2 as follows
Next row Reading chart 2 from right to left, k across 1st row, patt to last 10 sts, reading chart 2 from left to right, k across 1st row.
Cont working from charts as set, inc one st at each end of 2nd row and foll 4th row, working inc sts into A. 84 sts. Patt 21 rows straight, working sts in MC when chart 1 has been completed.
Dec one st at each end of next row and 3 foll 4th rows. 76 sts. Patt 1 row.
Place chart 3 as follows
Next row Patt 11, reading chart 3 from right to left, k across 1st row, k2MC, reading chart 3 from left to right, k across 1st row, patt 11.
Cont working from charts as set, patt 3

rows, thus completing chart 2.
Shape Front Legs
Cast on 4 sts at beg of next 6 rows and 10 sts at beg of foll 2 rows. 120 sts. Patt 14 rows straight. Cast off 22 sts at beg of next 2 rows. 76 sts. Dec one st at each end of 5th row and every foll alt row until 52 sts rem. Patt 1 row. Cast off 2 sts at beg of next 2 rows. Patt 1 row. Mark each end of last row.
Shape Head
Next row Patt 16, cast off next 16 sts, patt to end.
Work on last set of 16 sts only for right side of head. Inc one st at beg of next row and 3 foll alt rows, **at the same time**, cast off 2 sts at beg of 4 foll alt rows. 12 sts.
Cont in MC only. Dec one st at end of 3rd row, then at each end of 3 foll 4th rows. K 2 rows. Mark each end of last row. Inc one st at beg of next row. K 1 row.
Cast off.
With right side facing, rejoin yarn at inside edge to rem sts for left side of head. Complete to match right side, reversing shapings.

UNDERSIDE
With MC, cast on 3 sts. Mark centre st. Work in garter st, inc one st at each end of 3rd row, foll 6th row, foll 8th row, then foll 10th row and foll 14th row. 13 sts. K 5 rows. Leave these sts on a holder.
Left Back Leg
Work as given for Left Back Leg of Upper Body.
Right Back Leg
Work as given for Right Back Leg of Upper Body.
Next row K across sts of Right Back Leg, k13 sts from holder, k across sts of Left Back Leg. 75 sts.
K 3 rows. Cast off 13 sts at beg of next 2 rows. 49 sts.
Next row K2 tog, k16, k2 tog tbl, k9, k2

Chart 2

Chart 3

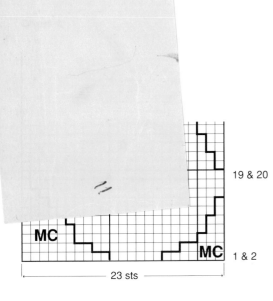

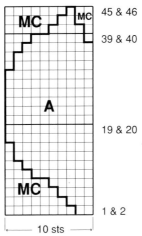

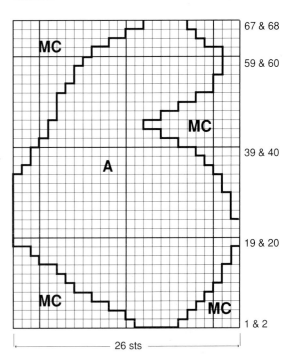

KEY

☐ 1 st and 2 rows

tog, k16, k2 tog.
K 1 row.
Next row K2 tog, k14, k2 tog tbl, k9, k2 tog, k14, k2 tog.
K 1 row.
Next row K2 tog, k12, k2 tog tbl, k9, k2 tog, k12, k2 tog.
Cont in this way, dec 4 sts as set on every alt row until 21 sts rem. Dec one st at each end of 2 foll alt rows, then at each end of next 2 rows. 13 sts.
Inc one st at each end of 4 foll 6th rows. 21 sts. K 27 rows straight. Dec one st at each end of next row and 3 foll 4th rows. 13 sts. K 3 rows.
Shape Front Legs
Cast on 4 sts at beg of next 6 rows and 10 sts at beg of foll 2 rows. 57 sts. K 14 rows. Cast off 22 sts at beg of next 2 rows. 13 sts.
Dec one st at each end of 7th row and 3 foll 6th rows. 5 sts. K 9 rows. Mark each end of last row. Inc one st at each end of next row and foll alt row, then on 2 foll 4th rows. 13 sts. Dec one st at each end of 2 foll 4th rows. K 3 rows.
Cast off 2 sts at beg of next 2 rows. 5 sts. K 2 rows. Mark each end of last row. Inc one st at each end of next row. 7 sts. K 13 rows. Dec one st at each end of next row. Mark each end of last row. Inc one st at each end of 6 foll 4th rows. 17 sts. K 5 rows. Cast off.

UDDER
With MC, cast on 46 sts.
Next 2 rows K3, turn, p to end.
Next 2 rows K6, turn, p to end.
Next 2 rows K10, turn, p to end.
Next 2 rows K16, turn, p to end.

Next row K to end.
Next 2 rows P3, turn, k to end.
Next 2 rows P6, turn, k to end.
Next 2 rows P10, turn, k to end.
Next 2 rows P16, turn, k to end.
Beg with a p row, work 5 rows in st st across all sts.
Next row K1, [k2 tog, k3] to end.
Work 3 rows straight.
Next row K1, [k2 tog, k2] to end.
Work 1 row.
Next row K1, [k2 tog, k1] to end.
Work 1 row.
Next row K1, [k2 tog] to end. 10 sts.
Break off yarn, thread end through rem sts, pull up and secure.

TEATS (make 4)
With Pink, cast on 5 sts. Beg with a k row, work 6 rows in st st.
Next row K1, [k2 tog] twice.
Break off yarn, thread end through rem sts, pull up and secure, then join seam.

EARS (make 2)
With MC, cast on 5 sts. K 10 rows. Dec one st at each end of next row. K3 tog and fasten off.

HORNS (make 2)
With Brown, cast on 4 sts. Beg with a k row, work 4 rows in st st.
Next row [K2 tog] twice.
Break off yarn, thread end through rem sts, pull up and secure, then join seam.

TAIL
With MC, cast on 30 sts. Cast off.

TO MAKE UP
Join upper body to underside, matching legs and markers and leaving an opening. Stuff and close opening. Join back seam of udder, stuff and sew in place. Sew teats to udder. Sew ears and horns in position. With MC, work fringe along top of head. With Black, embroider eyes. Make small tassel with MC and attach to one end of tail. Attach other end to body.

Bull

UPPER BODY, UNDERSIDE AND EARS
Work as given for Upper Body, Underside and Ears of Cow using MC throughout.

HORNS (make 2)
With Brown, cast on 6 sts. Beg with a k row, work 6 rows in st st. Dec one st at each end of next row and foll alt row. Work 1 row. K2 tog and fasten off.

TAIL
With MC, cast on 30 sts. Cast off.

TO MAKE UP
Join upper body to underside, matching legs and markers and leaving an opening. Stuff and close opening. Join seam of horns and sew them in place. Sew on ears. With MC, work fringe along top of head. With Brown, embroider eyes. Make small tassel with MC and attach to one end of tail. Attach other end to body. Attach ring to end of nose.

Donkey

See Page
21

MATERIALS
3 × 25g hanks of Rowan Lightweight DK in Grey (A).
Small amount of same in Black (B).
Pair of 3¼mm (No 10/US 3) knitting needles. Stuffing.

MEASUREMENTS
Approximately 19cm/7½in high and 28cm/11in long.

TENSION
28 sts and 36 rows to 10cm/4in square over st st.

ABBREVIATIONS
See page 10.

UPPER BODY
** With A, cast on 13 sts for left leg. Beg with a k row, work in st st, inc one st at end of 2nd row and at same edge on every row until there are 20 sts. Leave these sts on a holder. **
With A, cast on 20 sts for centre. Mark 5th st from each end. Beg with a k row, work 2 rows in st st. Cont in st st, casting on 8 sts at beg of next 4 rows. 52 sts. Leave these sts on a holder.
*** With A, cast on 13 sts for right leg. Beg with a k row, work in st st, inc one st at beg of 2nd row and at same edge on every row until there are 20 sts. ***
Next row K to end, then k25, m1, k2, m1, k25 across centre sts, k left leg sts. 94 sts. Work 3 rows.
Next row K46, m1, k2, m1, k46.
Work 1 row straight. Cast off 8 sts at beg of next 2 rows.
Next row K2 tog, k37, m1, k2, m1, k37, k2 tog. 80 sts.
Dec one st at each end of next 8 rows. 64 sts. Work 3 rows. Inc one st at each end of next row and foll 4th row. 68 sts. Work 11 rows. Dec one st at each end of next row and foll 4th row. 64 sts. Work 3 rows.
Shape Front Legs
Cast on 5 sts at beg of next 4 rows and 7 sts at beg of foll 2 rows. 98 sts. Work 10 rows. Cast off 8 sts at beg of next 4 rows and 4 sts at beg of foll 2 rows. 58 sts. Dec one st at each end of next 4 rows.
Shape Head
Next row Cast off 3 sts, k20 sts more, m1, k2, m1, k24.
Cast off 3 sts at beg of next row.
Next row K2 tog, k20, m1, k2, m1, k20, k2 tog.
Mark each end of last row. P 1 row.
Next row Cast on 3 sts, k25, m1, k2, m1, k22.
Cast on 3 sts at beg of next row.
Next row Cast on 4 sts, k30, m1, k2,

m1, k26.
Cast on 4 sts at beg of next row. 64 sts.
Next row K twice in first st, k30, m1, k2, m1, k30, k twice in last st.
Inc one st at each end of next row.
Next row K twice in first st, k33, m1, k2, m1, k33, k twice in last st.
Inc one st at each end of next row. 76 sts.
Next row K twice in first st, k30, turn. Work on this set of sts only for side of

Next row P to last st, inc in last st.
Cast off 16 sts at beg of next row marking 7th st from beg.
Cast off 3 sts at beg of next row and 10 sts at beg of foll row. Cast off rem 4 sts. With right side facing, slip centre 14 sts onto a holder, rejoin yarn to rem sts, k to last st, inc in last st. Cast off 15 sts at beg of next row marking 6th st from beg.
Cast off 3 sts at beg of next row and 10 sts at beg of foll row. Work 1 row. Cast off rem 4 sts.
With right side facing, rejoin yarn to centre sts for head gusset.
Next row K7, m1, k7. 15 sts. P 1 row.
Inc one st at each end of next row. Work 3 rows. Dec one st at each end of next row and foll alt row. 13 sts. Work 3 rows. Inc one st at each end of next row and foll alt row. Work 1 row.
Next row K twice in first st, k7, m1, k1, m1, k7, k twice in last st. Work 1 row.
Next row K twice in first st, k9, m1, k1, m1, k9, k twice in last st.
Inc one st at each end of foll alt row. 27 sts. Work 7 rows. Dec one st at each end of next 2 rows.
Next row K2 tog, k7, skpo, k1, k2 tog, k7, k2 tog.
Mark each end of last row.
Next row P2 tog, p5, p2 tog, p1, p2 tog tbl, p5, p2 tog.
Next row K2 tog, k3, skpo, k1, k2 tog, k3, k2 tog.
Next row P2 tog, p1, p2 tog, p1, p2 tog tbl, p1, p2 tog.
Cast off, dec at centre as before.

UNDERSIDE
Work as given for Upper Body from ** to **.
With A, cast on 3 sts for centre. Beg with a k row, work in st st, inc one st at each end of 3rd row and 4 foll 4th rows. 13 sts. Work 3 rows. Leave these sts on a holder. Work as given for Upper Body from *** to ***.
Next row K to end, then k1, skpo, k7, k2 tog, k1 across centre sts, k left leg sts. 51 sts. Work 1 row.
Next row K21, skpo, k5, k2 tog, k21. Work 1 row.
Next row K21, skpo, k3, k2 tog, k21. Work 1 row.
Next row Cast off 8, k12 sts more, skpo, k1, k2 tog, k21.

Cast off 8 sts at beg of next row.
Next row K2 tog, k11, sl 1, k2 tog, psso, k11, k2 tog.
Dec one st at each end of next row.
Next row K2 tog, k9, m1, k1, m1, k9, k2 tog.
Dec one st at each end of next row.
Next row K2 tog, k7, m1, k3, m1, k7, k2 tog.
Dec one st at each end of next row.
Next row K2 tog, k5, [m1, k5] twice, k2 tog.
Dec one st at each end of next row.
Next row K2 tog, k3, m1, k7, m1, k3, k2 tog. 17 sts.
Inc one st at each end of 2 foll 4th rows. Work 11 rows. Dec one st at each end of next row and foll 4th row. Work 3 rows.
Shape Front Legs
Cast on 5 sts at beg of next 2 rows.
Next row Cast on 5 sts, k14, skpo, k5, k2 tog, k9.
Cast on 5 sts at beg of next row.
Next row Cast on 7 sts, k21, skpo, k3, k2 tog, k14.
Cast on 7 sts at beg of next row. 47 sts.
Next row K21, skpo, k1, k2 tog, k21. Work 1 row.
Next row K21, sl 1, k2 tog, psso, k21. Work 3 rows.
Next row K21, m1, k1, m1, k21. Work 1 row.
Next row K21, m1, k3, m1, k21. Work 1 row.
Next row Cast off 8 sts, k12 sts more, m1, k5, m1, k21.
Cast off 8 sts at beg of next row.
Next row Cast off 8 sts, k4 sts more, m1, k7, m1, k13.
Cast off 8 sts at beg of next row and 4 sts at beg of foll 2 rows. 11 sts.
Dec one st at each end of 3rd row and every foll alt row until 3 sts rem.
Work 3 tog and fasten off.

EARS (make 4)
With A, cast on 9 sts. Beg with a k row, work 2 rows in st st.
Next row K4, m1, k1, m1, k4. P1 row.
Next row K twice in first st, k4, m1, k1, m1, k4, k twice in last st.
Cont in st st, inc one st at each end of 2nd row and foll 4th row. 19 sts. Work 9 rows straight. Dec one st at each end of next row and every foll alt row until 3 sts rem. Work 3 tog and fasten off.

TAIL
With A, cast on 22 sts. Work 8 rows in st st. Cast off.

TO MAKE UP
Fold upper body in half and join cast on edge of centre back together to markers, then join underchin seam from markers to cast off edge of head. Sew head gusset in, matching markers. Join upper body to underside, matching legs and leaving an

opening. Stuff firmly and close opening. With right sides together, join paired ear pieces together, leaving cast on edge free. Turn to right side and close opening. Fold this edge in half and sew in place. Fold tail widthwise and join cast on and cast off edges together. With B, make a small pompon and attach to one end of tail. Sew other end in place. Cut B yarn into short strands. With long length of B yarn, tie five short strands together at centre. Place centre of five more strands where the knot is and tie them together. Continue in this way until mane is required length. Sew in place. With B, embroider eyes, nostrils and mouth.

Teddy Bear with Smock

See Page 22

MATERIALS
Teddy Bear 5×25g hanks of Rowan Lightweight DK in Brown (A).
Small amount of same in Black (B).
Pair of 3¼mm (No 10/US 3) knitting needls. Stuffing.
Smock 2×50g balls of Rowan Californian Cotton.
Pair of 3¾mm (No 9/US 4) knitting needles.
4 buttons. Cable needle.

MEASUREMENTS
Teddy Bear Approximately 41cm/16in high.
Smock Actual chest measurement 41cm/16in
Length 23cm/9in
Sleeve seam 11cm/4¼in

TENSION
28 sts and 36 rows to 10cm/4in square over st st using Lightweight DK and 3¼mm (No 10/US 3) needles.
23 sts and 32 rows to 10cm/4in square over st st using Californian Cotton and 3¾mm (No 9/US 4) needles.
30 sts and 30 rows to 10cm/4in square over cable pattern using Californian Cotton and 3¾mm (No 9/US 4) needles.

ABBREVIATIONS
C2B = slip next st onto cable needle and leave at back of work, p1, then p st from cable needle;
C2F = slip next st onto cable needle and leave at front of work, k1, then k st from cable needle;
Cr2L = slip next st onto cable needle and leave at front of work, p1, then k st from cable needle;
Cr2R = slip next st onto cable needle and leave at back of work, k1, then p st from cable needle.
Also see page 10.

Teddy Bear

RIGHT LEG
With A, cast on 24 sts. P 1 row.
Next row K1, [m1, k2] to last st, m1, k1. P 1 row.
Next row K9, [m1, k1] 3 times, [k1, m1] 3 times, k12, [m1, k1] 3 times, [k1, m1] 3 times, k3. P 1 row.
Next row K12, [m1, k2] 4 times, k16, [m1, k2] 4 times, k4. 56 sts.
Work 13 rows in st st.
Next row K11, cast off next 12 sts, k to end. Work across all sts.
Next row P30, p2 tog tbl, p2, p2 tog, p8.
Next row K7, k2 tog, k2, skpo, k16, skpo, k1, k2 tog, k8.
Next row P7, p2 tog, p1, p2 tog tbl, p26. 36 sts.
** Work 6 rows. Inc one st at each end of next row and 2 foll 4th rows. 42 sts. Work 13 rows.
Next row K8, k2 tog, k1, skpo, k16, k2 tog, k1, skpo, k8.
Work 3 rows.
Next row K7, k2 tog, k1, skpo, k14, k2 tog, k1, skpo, k7.

Work 1 row.
Next row K6, k2 tog, k1, skpo, k12, k2 tog, k1, skpo, k6.
Work 1 row.
Next row K5, k2 tog, k1, skpo, k10, k2 tog, k1, skpo, k5.
Work 1 row.
Next row K4, k2 tog, k1, skpo, k8, k2 tog, k1, skpo, k4.
Next row P3, p2 tog tbl, p1, p2 tog, p6, p2 tog tbl, p1, p2 tog, p3.
Next row K2, k2 tog, k1, skpo, k4, k2 tog, k1, skpo, k2. 14 sts. Cast off.
Join instep, top and inner leg seam, leaving cast on edge free. Stuff firmly and join sole seam.

LEFT LEG
With A, cast on 24 sts. P 1 row.
Next row K1, [m1, k2] to last st, m1, k1. P 1 row.
Next row K3, [m1, k1] 3 times, [k1, m1] 3 times, k12, [m1, k1] 3 times, [k1, m1] 3 times, k9. P 1 row.
Next row K6, [m1, k2] 4 times, k16, [m1, k2] 4 times, k10. 56 sts.
Work 13 rows in st st.
Next row K33, cast off next 12 sts, k to end. Work across all sts.

Next row P8, p2 tog tbl, p2, p2 tog, p30.
Next row K8, skpo, k1, k2 tog, k16, k2 tog, k2, skpo, k7.
Next row P26, p2 tog, p1, p2 tog tbl, p7. 36 sts.
Complete as given for Right Leg from ** to end.

BODY
Begin at neck edge.
With A, cast on 24 sts. P 1 row.
Next row K1, [m1, k2] to last st, m1, k1. P 1 row.
Next row K2, [m1, k3] to last st, m1, k1. 48 sts. Work 7 rows in st st.
Next row K10, m1, k1, m1, k2, m1, k1, m1, k9, m1, k2, m1, k9, m1, k1, m1, k2, m1, k1, m1, k10.
Work 5 rows.
Next row K11, [m1, k2] 4 times, k9, m1, k2, m1, k11, [m1, k2] 4 times, k9.
P 1 row.
Next row K12, m1, k3, m1, k2, m1, k3, m1, k28, m1, k3, m1, k2, m1, k3, m1, k12. 76 sts.
Work 5 rows.
Next row K17, m1, k2, m1, k38, m1, k2, m1, k17.
Work 5 rows
Next row K18, m1, k2, m1, k40, m1, k2, m1, k18.
Work 5 rows.
Next row K19, m1, k2, m1, k42, m1, k2, m1, k19. 88 sts.
Work 19 rows.
Next row K18, k2 tog, k2, skpo, k40, k2 tog, k2, skpo, k18.
P 1 row.
Next row K17, k2 tog, k2, skpo, k38, k2 tog, k2, skpo, k17.
P 1 row.
Next row K16, k2 tog, k2, skpo, k36, k2 tog, k2, skpo, k16.
P 1 row.
Next row K10, k2 tog, k3, k2 tog, k2, skpo, k3, skpo, k24, k2 tog, k3, k2 tog, k2, skpo, k3, skpo, k10.
P 1 row.
Next row K9, [k2 tog, k2] twice, [skpo, k2] twice, k6, skpo, k2, k2 tog, k8, [k2 tog, k2] twice, [skpo, k2] twice, k7.
P 1 row.
Next row K8, [k2 tog, k1] twice, [k1, skpo] twice, k6, skpo, k2, k2 tog, k6, [k2 tog, k1] twice, [k1, skpo] twice, k8.
P 1 row.

Next row K1, [k2 tog, k2] 3 times, [skpo, k2] 3 times, [k2 tog, k2] 3 times, [skpo, k2] twice, skpo, k1.
P 1 row.
Next row [K2 tog, k1] to end. 24 sts.
Cast off.

ARMS (make 2)
With A, cast on 15 sts. P 1 row.
Next row K1, [m1, k2] to end. 22 sts.
Beg with a p row, work in st st, inc one st at each end of 4 foll alt rows, then on every foll 4th row until there are 40 sts. Work 19 rows straight.
Next row K7, k2 tog, k2, skpo, k14, k2 tog, k2, skpo, k7.
Work 3 rows.
Next row K6, k2 tog, k2, skpo, k12, k2 tog, k2, skpo, k6.
Work 1 row.
Next row K5, k2 tog, k2, skpo, k10, k2 tog, k2, skpo, k5.
Work 1 row.
Next row K4, k2 tog, k2, skpo, k8, k2 tog, k2, skpo, k4.
Next row P3, p2 tog tbl, p2, p2 tog, p6, p2 tog tbl, p2, p2 tog, p3.
Next row K2, k2 tog, skpo, k4, k2 tog, k2, skpo, k2.
Cast off.
Join top and underarm seam, leaving an opening. Stuff firmly and close opening.

HEAD
Begin at neck edge.
With A, cast on 24 sts. Beg with a k row, work 4 rows in st st.
Next row K1, [m1, k2] to last st, m1, k1.
Work 3 rows.
Next row K2, [m1, k3] to last st, m1, k1.
Work 3 rows.
Next row Cast on 4 sts, k7, [m1, k4] to last st, m1, k1.
Cast on 4 sts at beg of next 5 rows. 84 sts. Work 14 rows. Mark each end of last row. Cast off 9 sts at beg of next 2 rows. Dec one st at each end of next 5 rows, then on 3 foll alt rows. 50 sts. P 1 row.
Next row K18, [skpo, k2] twice, [k2 tog, k2] twice, k3, skpo, turn.
Next row Sl 1, p20, p2 tog, turn.
Next row Sl 1, k20, skpo, turn.
Next row Sl 1, p20, p2 tog, turn.
Rep last 2 rows 3 times more.
Next row Sl 1, k20, sl 1, k2 tog, psso, turn.
Next row Sl 1, p20, p3 tog, turn.
Next row Sl 1, k20, skpo, turn.
Next row Sl 1, p20, p2 tog, turn.
Rep last 2 rows 4 times more. Work on rem 22 sts for gusset. Dec one st at each end of 5th row and foll 4th row, then on 2 foll alt rows. P 1 row.
Next row K2 tog, k2, skpo, [k2, k2 tog] twice. 10 sts.
Work 7 rows. Dec one st at each end of every row until 2 sts rem. Work 2 tog and fasten off.
Sew in gusset to markers. Join snout and underchin seam, leaving cast on edge free. Stuff firmly. Run gathering thread along cast on edge, pull up and secure.

EARS (make 4)
With A, cast on 20 sts. Beg with a k row, work in st st, dec one st at each end of 7th row, foll 4th row, then on 2 foll alt rows. Dec one st at each end of next row. 10 sts. Cast off.

NOSE
With B, cast on 9 sts. Beg with a k row, work in st st, dec one st at each end of 3rd row and every foll alt row until 3 sts rem. Work 1 row. K 3 tog and fasten off.

TO MAKE UP
Fold sides of body to centre, then join cast off edge together. Join back seam of body. Stuff firmly. Run gathering thread along cast on edge, pull up and secure. Sew head in place. Join paired ear pieces together and sew them in place. Sew on nose. With Black, embroider mouth and eyes. Attach yarn at seam about 1cm/¼in below top of one arm, thread through body at shoulder position, then attach other arm, pull up yarn tightly and thread through body again in same place, then attach yarn to first arm again and fasten off. Attach legs at lower edge of body in same way as arms.

Smock

BACK
Cast on 63 sts. K 5 rows.
Next row K7, [k twice in next st, k11] 4 times, k twice in next st, k7. 68 sts.
Beg with a p row, work in st st until Back measures 14cm/5½in from beg, ending with a k row.
Next row P5, [p2 tog, p3] to last 3 sts, p3. 56 sts.
Work in cable patt as follows:
1st row (right side) P3, [C2F, p4] to last 5 sts, C2F, p3.
2nd row K2, [Cr2L, Cr2R, k2] to end.
3rd row P1, [Cr2R, p2, Cr2L] to last st, p1.
4th row K1, p1, [k4, C2B] to last 6 sts, k4, p1, k1.
5th row P1, [Cr2L, p2, Cr2R] to last st, p1.
6th row K2, [Cr2R, Cr2L, k2] to end.
These 6 rows form cable patt. Cont in patt until Back measures 22cm/8¾in from beg, ending with a right side row.
Shape Neck
Next row Patt 21, cast off next 14 sts, patt to end.
Work on last set of sts only. Dec one st at neck edge on next 2 rows.
Cast off rem 19 sts.
With right side facing, rejoin yarn to rem sts. Dec one st at neck edge on next 2 rows. Cast off rem 19 sts.

LEFT FRONT
Cast on 36 sts. K 5 rows.
Next row K5, [k twice in next st, k11] twice, k twice in next st, k6. 39 sts.
Next row K2, p to end.
Next row K.
Rep last 2 rows until Front measures 14cm/5½in from beg, ending with a right

side row.
Next row K2, p5, [p2 tog, p3] to last 2 sts, p2. 33 sts.
Next row P3, [C2F, p4] to last 6 sts, C2F, p2, k2.
Next row K3, [Cr2L, Cr2R, k2] to end.
These 2 rows set position of cable patt. Cont in patt as set until Front measures 20cm/8in from beg, ending at front edge.
Shape Neck
Keeping patt correct, cast off 8 sts at beg of next row and 3 sts at beg of 2 foll alt rows. 19 sts. Work few rows straight until Front matches Back to cast off edge, ending with a wrong side row. Cast off.
Mark front edge to indicate position for 4 buttons: first one 9cm/3½in up from lower edge, last one 1cm/¼in below neck edge and rem 2 evenly spaced between.

RIGHT FRONT
Cast on 36 sts. K 5 rows.
Next row K6, [k twice in next st, k11] twice, k twice in next st, k5. 39 sts.
Next row P to last 2 sts, k2.
Next row K.
Rep last 2 rows until Front measures 14cm/5½in from beg, ending with a right side row, **at the same time**, make button-holes to match markers on Left Front as follows:
Buttonhole row K2, yf, k2 tog, patt to end.
Next row P5, [p2 tog, p3] to last 4 sts, p2, k2. 33 sts.
Next row K2, p2, [C2F, p4] to last 5 sts, C2F, p3.
Next row [K2, Cr2L, Cr2R] to last 3 sts, k3.
These 2 rows set position of cable patt. Cont in patt as set, complete to match Left Front, making buttonholes to match markers as before.

SLEEVES
Cast on 44 sts. K 3 rows. Work 7 rows of cable patt as given for Back.
Next row P7, [p twice in next st, p5] to last st, p1. 50 sts.
Beg with a k row, work 12 rows in st st, inc one st at each end of 3rd row and 2 foll 4th rows. 56 sts.
Next row K15, work 1st row of cable patt across next 26 sts, k15.
Next row P15, work 2nd row of cable patt across next 26 sts, p15.
These 2 rows set position of cable patt. Cont in patt as set until Sleeve measures 11cm/4¼in from beg, ending with a wrong side row. Cast off.

COLLAR
Cast on 42 sts. K 3 rows.
Next row K2, p3, C2F, p3, k5, k twice in next st, k10, k twice in next st, k5, p3, C2F, p3, k2. 44 sts.
Work in patt as follows:
1st row (wrong side) K4, Cr2L, Cr2R, k2, p24, k2, Cr2L, Cr2R, k4.
2nd row K2, p1, Cr2R, p2, Cr2L, p1, k24, p1, Cr2R, p2, Cr2L, p1, k2.
3rd row K3, p1, k4, p1, k1, p24, k1, p1, k4, p1, k3.
4th row K2, p1, Cr2L, p2, Cr2R, p1, k24, p1, Cr2L, p2, Cr2R, p1, k2.
5th row K4, Cr2R, Cr2L, k2, p24, k2,

Cr2R, Cr2L, k4.
6th row K2, p3, C2F, p3, k24, p3, C2F, p3, k2.
These 6 rows form patt. Patt 9 rows more.
Next row Patt 17, cast off next 10 sts, patt to end.
Work on last set of sts only for left side of front collar. Dec one st at inside edge on next 2 rows. Patt 4 rows straight. Inc one st at inside edge on next 5 rows. Cast on 4 sts at beg of next row. 24 sts.
Next row Patt to last 2 sts, k2.
Next row K2, patt to end.

Rep last 2 rows 3 times more. K 2 rows, dec one st at centre of cable patt on first row. Cast off knitwise.
With wrong side facing, rejoin yarn to rem sts, patt to last 2 sts, k2. Dec one st at inside edge on next 2 rows. Patt 4 rows straight. Inc one st at inside edge on next 5 rows. Cast on 4 sts at beg of next row.
Next row Patt to end.
Next row K2, patt to end.
Rep last 2 rows twice more, then work first of the 2 rows again. K 2 rows, dec one st at centre of cable patt on first row. Cast

off knitwise.

POCKETS (make 2)
Cast on 12 sts. Beg with a k row, work 11 rows in st st. K 2 rows. Cast off knitwise.

TO MAKE UP
Join shoulder seams. Sew on sleeves, placing centre of sleeves to shoulder seams. Join side and sleeve seams. Sew on pockets and buttons. Beginning in line with buttonholes and ending in line with buttons, sew on collar.

Girl Rabbit

See Page
25

MATERIALS
2 × 25g hanks of Rowan 4 ply Botany in Cream (A) and 3 hanks in Purple (B).
Oddment of Brown yarn for embroidery.
Pair each of 2¾mm (No 12/US 1) and 3¼mm (No 10/US 3) knitting needles.
Medium size crochet hook.
1 button.
Shirring elastic.
Stuffing.

MEASUREMENTS
Rabbit Approximately 32cm/12½in high.
Dress Actual chest measurement

23cm/9in
Length 18cm/7in
Sleeve seam 6cm/2½in

TENSION
34 sts and 46 rows to 10cm/4in square over st st on 2¾mm (No 12/US 1) needles.
28 sts and 36 rows to 10cm/4in square over st st using two strands of yarn together on 3¼mm (No 10/US 3) needles.

ABBREVIATIONS
See page 10.

Rabbit

Using 2¾mm (No 12/US 1) needles and A throughout, work as given for Rabbit of Farmer Rabbits (see overleaf), but working 49 rows across all sts on legs instead of 59 rows and inc one st at each end of 6th row and 4 foll 6th rows instead of 8th rows on arms. Embroider face features with Brown instead of Pink.

Dress

SKIRT (make 2)
With 3¼mm (No 10/US 3) needles and using two strands of B yarn together, cast on 58 sts. K 3 rows. Beg with a k row, work 38 rows in st st.
Next row K3, [k2 tog] to last 3 sts, k3. 32 sts. P 1 row. Cast off.

FRONT BODICE
With 3¼mm (No 10/US 3) needles and using two strands of B yarn together, cast on 32 sts. Beg with a k row, work 20 rows in st st.
Shape Neck
**Next 2 rows K12, turn, sl 1, p to end.
Next 2 rows K10, turn, sl 1, p to end.
Next 2 rows K8, turn, sl 1, p to end.
Next row K to end. **
***Next 2 rows P12, turn, sl 1, k to end.
Next 2 rows P10, turn, sl 1, k to end.
Next 2 rows P8, turn, sl 1, k to end.
Next row P to end. ***
Cast off.

BACK BODICE
With 3¼mm (No 10/US 3) needles and using two strands of B yarn together, cast on 32 sts. Beg with a k row, work 4 rows in st st.

Divide for Opening
Next row K16, turn.
Next row K2, p14.
Next row K.
Rep last 2 rows 6 times more, then work first of the 2 rows again.
Now work as given for Front Bodice from ** to **. Work 1 row. Cast off.
With right side facing, rejoin yarn to rem sts and k to end.
Next row P14, k2.
Next row K.
Rep last 2 rows 7 times more. Now work as given for Front Bodice from *** to ***
Cast off.

SLEEVES
Join first and last 8 sts of cast off row of Back and Front Bodices for shoulders. Beginning and ending 5 rows up from cast on edges, pick up and k 36 sts evenly along side edge.
Next row P13, [p twice in next st] 10 times, p13. 46 sts.
Beg with a k row, work 16 rows in st st.
Next row K1, [k3 tog] to end.
P 1 row.
Next row K1, [k into front, back and front of next st] to end.
Beg with a p row, work 2 rows in st st. K 1 row. Cast off.

TO MAKE UP
Sew cast off edge of skirt to bodice. Join side and sleeve seams. With crochet hook, make a buttonhole loop at the top of left side of back opening, sew button to other side. Thread length of shirring elastic on wrong side along p row between increase and decrease rows on sleeves, pull up slightly and tie ends together.

Farmer Rabbits

See Page
23/24

MATERIALS
Rabbit 4×25g hanks of Rowan Lightweight DK.
Oddment of Pink yarn for embroidery.
Pair of 3¼mm (No 10/US 3) knitting needles.
Stuffing.
Dress 2×25g hanks of Rowan 4 ply Botany in each of two contrasting colours (A and B).
Pair each of 2¾mm (No 12/US 1) and 3mm (No 11/US 2) knitting needles.
Medium size crochet hook.
1 button. Shirring elastic.
Apron 1×25g hank of Rowan 4 ply Botany.
Pair of 3¼mm (No 10/US 3) knitting needles.
Length of string.
Dungarees 3×25g hanks of Rowan 4 ply Botany.
Length of Silver lurex yarn.
Pair of 3¼mm (No 10/US 3) knitting needles.
Hat Small amount of Rowan Californian Cotton.

Pair of 4mm (No 8/US 6) knitting needles.

MEASUREMENTS
Rabbit Approximately 42cm/16½in high.
Dress Actual chest measurement 32cm/12½in
Length 27cm/10¾in
Sleeve seam 13cm/5in
Dungarees Actual hip measurement 40cm/16in
Length 30cm/11¾in
Inside leg seam 14cm/5½in

TENSION
28 sts and 36 rows to 10cm/4in square over st st using DK yarn or using two strands of 4 ply yarn together on 3¼mm (No 10/US 3) needles.
34 sts and 54 rows to 10cm/4in square over pattern using 4 ply yarn and 3mm (No 11/US 2) needles.

ABBREVIATIONS
See page 10.

Rabbit

LEGS (make 2)
Cast on 22 sts. P 1 row.
Next row [K twice in next st] to end.
P 1 row.
Next row [K1, m1] twice, k18, [m1, k1] 5 times, k17, [m1, k1] twice. 53 sts.
Beg with a p row, work 7 rows in st st.
Next row K24, k2 tog, k1, skpo, k24.
P 1 row.
Next row K23, k2 tog, k1, skpo, k23.
P 1 row.
Next row K22, k2 tog, k1, skpo, k22.
P 1 row.
Next row K14, cast off next 19 sts, k to end. 28 sts.
Work 59 rows in st st across all sts.
Cast off.
Join back leg seam, sole seam and instep seam. Stuff foot firmly, easing stuffing along the leg. Close opening.

ARMS (make 2)
Cast on 9 sts. P 1 row.
Next row K1, [m1, k1] to end.
P 1 row.
Next row K7, [m1, k1] 3 times, k7.
P 1 row.
Next row K9, [m1, k1] twice, k9. 22 sts.
Work 9 rows in st st.
Next row [K2 tog, k7, skpo] twice. 18 sts.
Cont in st st, inc one st at each end of 6th row and 4 foll 8th rows. 28 sts.
Work 11 rows straight. Cast off.
Join underarm seam. Stuff hand firmly,

easing stuffing along the arm.
Close opening.

BODY AND HEAD
Cast on 56 sts. P 1 row.
Next row K13, [m1, k1] 3 times, k12, m1, k13, [m1, k1] 3 times, k12.
P 1 row.
Next row K31, m1, k1, m1, k31.
P 1 row.
Next row K31, m1, k3, m1, k31.
P 1 row.
Next row K31, m1, k5, m1, k31. 69 sts.
Work 13 rows in st st.
Next row K13, k2 tog, k1, skpo, k33, k2 tog, k1, skpo, k13.
Work 5 rows.
Next row K12, k2 tog, k1, skpo, k31, k2 tog, k1, skpo, k12.
Work 5 rows.
Next row K11, k2 tog, k1, skpo, k29, k2 tog, k1, skpo, k11.
Work 5 rows.
Next row K10, k2 tog, k1, skpo, k11, skpo, k1, k2 tog, k11, k2 tog, k1, skpo, k10.
P 1 row.
Next row K23, skpo, k1, k2 tog, k23.
P 1 row.
Next row K22, skpo, k1, k2 tog, k22.
P 1 row.
Next row K9, k2 tog, k1, skpo, k7, skpo, k1, k2 tog, k7, k2 tog, k1, skpo, k9. 41 sts.
P 1 row.
Shape Head
Next row K20, m1, k1, m1, k20.
Work 5 rows.

Next row K1, [m1, k20, m1, k1] twice.
Work 3 rows.
Next row K23, m1, k1, m1, k23.
Next row P24, m1, p1, m1, p24.
Next row K1, [m1, k24, m1, k1] twice.
Next row P27, m1, p1, m1, p27. 57 sts.
Work 2 rows.
Next row K1, [skpo, k23, k2 tog, k1] twice.
Work 3 rows.
Next row K1, [skpo, k21, k2 tog, k1] twice.
P 1 row.
Next row K1, skpo, k5, skpo, k29, k2 tog, k5, k2 tog, k1.
P 1 row.
Next row K1, [skpo, k17, k2 tog, k1] twice.
P 1 row.
Next row K1, skpo, k3, skpo, k25, k2 tog, k3, k2 tog, k1.
P 1 row.
Next row K1, [skpo, k13, k2 tog, k1] twice.
P 1 row.
Next row [K1, skpo] twice, k8, k2 tog, k1, skpo, k8, [k2 tog, k1] twice.
27 sts. P 1 row. Cast off.

EARS (make 2)
Cast on 16 sts.
** **Next 2 rows** K2, sl 1, yf, turn, sl 1, k2.
Next 2 rows K4, sl 1, yf, turn, sl 1, k4.
Next 2 rows K6, sl 1, yf, turn, sl 1, k6.
Next 2 rows K7, sl 1, yf, turn, sl 1, k7.
K 1 row across all sts. **
Rep from ** to **. K 60 rows.
Next row K1, skpo, k to last 3 sts, k2 tog, k1.
K 3 rows. Rep last 4 rows once.
Next row K1, skpo, k to last 3 sts, k2 tog, k1.
K 1 row. Rep last 2 rows twice.
Next row K1, skpo, k2 tog, k1.
K 1 row.
Next row Skpo, k2 tog.
K2 tog and fasten off.

TO MAKE UP
Join back seam of body and head. Insert top of legs at lower edge and stitch in place. Stuff body and head. Close opening. Sew on arms.
Fold cast on edge of ears in half and stitch together, sew them in place.
With Pink, outline nose and embroider mouth pulling yarn tightly to form those features. Embroider eyes with Pink.

Dress

BACK
With 3mm (No 11/US 2) needles and A, cast on 108 sts. K 3 rows.
Work in patt as follows:
1st row (right side) With A, k1, [sl 1, p1, k2] to last 3 sts, sl 1, p1, k1.

2nd row With A, p to end.
3rd row With B, [sl 1, p1, k2] to end.
4th row With B, p to end.
These 4 rows form patt. Cont in patt until Back measures 17cm/6¾in from beg, ending with a wrong side row.
Dec row With A, [k2 tog] to end. 54 sts.
With A, k 3 rows. Mark each end of last row. **
Working first and last st in st st, work in patt for 2cm/¾in, ending with a wrong side row.

Divide for Opening
Next row Patt 27, turn.
Work on this set of sts only for a further 7cm/2¾in, ending with a wrong side row.
Leave these sts on a holder.
With right side facing, rejoin yarn to rem sts on needle and patt to end.
Complete as given for first side.

FRONT
Work as given for Back to **. Working first and last st in st st, work in patt for 9cm/3½in, ending with a wrong side row.
Leave these sts on a spare needle.

SLEEVES
With 3mm (No 11/US 2) needles and A, cast on 36 sts. K 3 rows.
Work in patt as given for Back for 2.5cm/1in, ending with a wrong side row.
Dec row With A, [k1, k2 tog] to end. 24 sts. With A, k 2 rows.
Inc row With A, k2, [m1, k1] to last 2 sts, k2. 44 sts.
Work in patt until Sleeve measures 13cm/5in from beg, ending with a wrong side row. Leave these sts on a spare needle.

NECKBAND
With right sides of Back and Front together, cast off 8 sts together at each end for shoulders.
With 2¾mm (No 12/US 1) needles, right side facing and A, k19 sts from left back neck, 38 sts from centre front, then k19 sts from right back neck. 76 sts. K 3 rows. Cast off.

BACK OPENING EDGINGS
With 2¾mm (No 12/US 1) needles, right side facing and A, pick up and k23 sts evenly along one edge, including neckband. K 1 row. Cast off.

ARMHOLE EDGINGS
With 3mm (No 11/US 2) needles, right

side facing and A, pick up and k44 sts evenly between markers. With right sides of Sleeves and body together, cast off together edging and top sleeve sts.

TO MAKE UP
Join side and sleeve seams. Thread length of shirring elastic along ridge between increase and decrease rows on wrong side of sleeves. Pull up slightly to fit Rabbit's wrist and tie ends together. With crochet hook, make buttonhole loop on top of left side of back opening, sew button to other side.

Apron

Begin at side edge.
Cast on 60 sts. K 3 rows.
Work in patt as follows:
1st row (right side) K to end.
2nd row K3, p54, k3.
3rd to 8th rows Rep 1st and 2nd rows 3 times.
9th and 10th rows K to end.
Rep last 10 rows 8 times more. K 2 rows. Cast off.
Place it on top of dress front on Rabbit.
Tie string around waist.

Dungarees

RIGHT LEG
Using 2 strands of yarn together, cast on 40 sts. K 3 rows.
Beg with a k row, work in st st, inc one st at each end of every foll 6th row until there are 56 sts. Work 2 rows. Mark each end of last row.
Work a further 19 rows. **
Next row P9 and slip these sts onto a safety pin for back bib, cast off next 33 sts, p to end. Leave rem 14 sts on a spare needle for front bib.

LEFT LEG
Work as given for Right Leg to **.
Next row P14 and slip these sts onto a spare needle for front bib, cast off next 33 sts, p to end. Leave rem 9 sts on a safety pin for back bib.

BIB POCKET LINING
Using 2 strands of yarn together, cast on 20 sts. Beg with a k row, work 17 rows in st st. Leave these sts on a holder.

FRONT BIB
With right side facing and using 2 strands of yarn together, rejoin yarn at inside edge of Left Leg front bib sts, k to end, then k Right Leg front bib sts. 28 sts. K 3 rows.
1st row K to end.
2nd row K2, p24, k2.
Rep last 2 rows 7 times more.
Next row K4, cast off next 20 sts, k to end.
Next row K2, p2, p across sts of pocket lining, p2, k2.
Rep 1st and 2nd rows once. K 4 rows.
Cast off.

BACK BIB
With right side facing and using 2 strands of yarn together, rejoin yarn at inside edge of Right Leg back bib sts, k to end, then k Left Leg back bib sts. 18 sts.
1st row K2, p to last 2 sts, k2.
2nd row K to end.
3rd and 4th rows As 1st and 2nd rows.
5th row As 1st row.
6th row K2, skpo, k to last 4 sts, k2 tog, k2.
Rep last 6 rows twice more, then work 1st to 5th rows again.
Next row K1, skpo, k6, k2 tog, k1.
Next row K1, p3, k1, turn.
Work on this set of sts only.
Next row K5.
Next row K1, p3, k1.
Rep last 2 rows until strap, when slightly stretched, fits over Rabbit shoulder to front bib, ending with a k row. K 3 rows.
Cast off.
With wrong side facing, rejoin yarn to rem sts, k1, p3, k1. Complete as for first strap.

TO MAKE UP
Join leg seams to markers, then join centre back and front seams. Catch down pocket lining. Divide pocket in half with back stitches. Sew end of straps to front bib. With lurex yarn, embroider buttons.

Hat

Cast on 22 sts. K 11 rows.
Next row [K twice in next st] to end.
44 sts. K 16 rows, inc one st at each end of 3 foll 4th rows. 50 sts. Thread 2 strands of yarn together through rem sts and secure ends. Gather cast on edge, pull up and secure. Join seam.

Gingham Bear

See Page
26

MATERIALS
4×25g hanks of Rowan Lightweight DK in each of Navy (A) and Cream (B). Pair of 3¼mm (No 10/US 3) knitting needles. Stuffing.

MEASUREMENTS
Approximately 43cm/17in high.

TENSION
30 sts and 30 rows to 10cm/4in square over pattern.

ABBREVIATIONS
See page 10.

BACK BODY
With A, cast on 108 sts. Mark 44th st from each end.
1st row (right side) K4A, [1B, 1A, 1B, 5A] to end.
2nd row P4A, [1B, 1A, 1B, 5A] to end.
3rd and 4th rows As 1st and 2nd rows. Mark each end of last row.
5th row [K1B, 1A] twice, [k5B, 1A, 1B, 1A] to end.
6th row [P1B, 1A] twice, [p5B, 1A, 1B, 1A] to end.
7th and 8th rows As 5th and 6th rows. These 8 rows form patt. Patt 12 rows more. Mark each end of last row. Work a further 12 rows. Cast off 28 sts at beg of next 2 rows. ** 52 sts. Patt 18 rows. Mark each end of last row. Work a further 8 rows in patt. Mark each end of last row.
Shape Legs
Cast on 3 sts at beg of next 2 rows. Mark 13th st from each end.
Keeping patt correct, cast on 3 sts at beg of foll 18 rows. 112 sts.
Mark each end of last row.
Next row Work 2 tog, patt 49, cast off next 10 sts, patt to last 2 sts, work 2 tog.
*** Work on last set of 50 sts.
Next row Work 2 tog, patt to end.
Next row Cast off 3, patt to last 2 sts, work 2 tog.

Rep last 2 rows until 5 sts rem. Cast off. With wrong side facing, rejoin yarn to rem sts.
Next row Cast off 3, patt to last 2 sts, work 2 tog.
Next row Work 2 tog, patt to end.
Rep last 2 rows until 5 sts rem. Cast off.

FRONT BODY
With A, cast on 124 sts. Mark 44th and 54th st from each end. Work as given for Back Body to **. 68 sts. Patt 18 rows.
Shape Legs
Cast on 3 sts at beg of foll 20 rows. 128 sts. Mark each end of last row.
Next row Work 2 tog, patt 49, cast off next 26 sts marking 5th and 21st of these sts, patt to last 2 sts, work 2 tog.
Complete as given for Back Body from *** to end.

FRONT HEAD
With A, cast on 36 sts. Work 2 rows in patt as given for Back Body. Keeping patt correct, cast on 8 sts at beg of next 8 rows. 100 sts. Patt 2 rows.
Next row Patt 34, turn.
Work on this set of sts only for side of head. Dec one st at beg of next row and at same edge on next 5 rows, then on 3 foll alt rows, ending with a wrong side row. 25 sts. Mark end of last row.
Next row Cast off 5, patt to last 2 sts, work 2 tog.
Patt 1 row. Dec one st at end of next row. Patt 1 row. Dec one st at each end of next row and every foll alt row until 8 sts rem, ending with a p row. Mark beg of last row. Cast off.
With right side facing, rejoin yarn to rem sts, patt 32, turn. Work on this set of sts only for centre gusset. Dec one st at each end of every foll alt row until 10 sts rem, then on every row until 2 sts rem. Work 2 tog and fasten off.
With right side facing, rejoin yarn to rem 34 sts for other side of head. Patt 1 row. Dec one st at end of next row and at same edge on next 5 rows, then on 4 foll alt rows. 24 sts. Mark end of last row. Cast off 5 sts at beg of next row. Dec one st at beg of next row. Patt 1 row. Dec one

st at each end of next row and every foll alt row until 8 sts rem, ending with a p row. Mark end of last row. Cast off.

BACK HEAD
With A, cast on 36 sts. Mark 14th st from each end. Work in patt as given for Back Body, inc one st at each end of 5th and 3 foll 4th rows. 44 sts. Patt 15 rows straight. Dec one st at each end of next row and 4 foll alt rows, then on every row until 28 sts rem. Mark 10th st from each end. Cast off.

SOLES (make 2)
With A, cast on 20 sts. Work 24 rows in patt as given for Back Body. Cast off.

EARS (make 2)
With A, cast on 20 sts. Work in patt as given for Back Body, dec one st at each end of 5th row, 2 foll alt rows then on every row until 8 sts rem. Cast off.

TO MAKE UP
Make darts at side edges of Back Body, using markers for guidance. Make darts about 20 rows long on top and between legs on Front Body, using centre markers. With right sides of back and front together, join shoulder and top of arm seam, tapering seam between markers. Sew seam straight until next marker is reached, then join underarm seam from marker to end of cast off sts for arm. Join side and top of leg seam to markers. Work other side in same way. Beginning at centre of last group of cast off sts, join inside leg and crotch seam. Sew in soles, tapering corners. Turn body to right side and stuff firmly. Run gathering thread around neck edge, pull up and secure. Join underchin and nose seam of head front between markers. Sew in centre gusset. Make darts about 12 rows long at top and bottom of head back, beginning at markers. Sew cast on edge of front head to back, leaving cast on edge of back free. Stuff firmly. Gather neck edge, pull up and secure. Sew head in place. Join paired ear pieces together and sew them in place.

Rag Head Doll

See Page
27

MATERIALS
Doll 3×25g hanks of Rowan Lightweight DK (A). 1×25g hank of Rowan 4 ply Botany (B).
Oddments of Brown or White yarn for embroidery. Stuffing.
Dress 2×25g hanks of Rowan 4 ply Botany in each of two contrasting colours (A and B). 2 buttons. Medium size crochet hook.
Pair of 3¼mm (No10/US 3) knitting needles.

MEASUREMENTS
Doll Approximately 37cm/14½in high.
Dress Actual chest measurement 26cm/10¼in
Length 25cm/10in
Sleeve seam 5cm/2in

TENSION
28 sts and 36 rows to 10cm/4in square over st st using DK yarn.
36 sts and 68 rows to 10cm/4in square over pattern using 4 ply yarn.

ABBREVIATIONS
See page 10.

Doll

LEGS (make 2)
With A, cast on 25 sts. Beg with a k row, work 58 rows in st st.
Next row [K2, k2 tog] 6 times, k1. P 1 row.
Next row [K1, k2 tog] 6 times, k1. P 1 row.
Next row [K2 tog] 6 times, k1.
Break off yarn. Thread end through rem sts, pull up and secure. Join inner leg seam. Stuff and close opening.

ARMS (make 2)
With A, cast on 28 sts. Beg with a k row, work in st st, dec one st at each end of 5th and foll 6th rows. Work 5 rows straight.
Next row K2 tog, [k9, k2 tog] twice.
Work 7 rows. Inc one st at each end of next 3 rows. Work 2 rows. Cast off 3 sts at beg of next 2 rows. Dec one st at each end of next row. Work 2 rows.
Next row K1, [k2 tog, k1] 6 times. P 1 row.
Next row K1, [k2 tog] 6 times.
Break off yarn. Thread end through rem sts, pull up and secure. Join underarm seam. Stuff and close opening.

BACK BODY
With A, cast on 25 sts. Beg with a k row, work 2 rows in st st.
Next row K twice in first st, [k7, k twice in next st] 3 times. P 1 row.
Next row K twice in first st, k to last st, k

twice in last st. 31 sts. **
Work 40 rows in st st.
Shape Neck
Next row P11, cast off next 9 sts, p to end.
Work on last set of sts only.
Next row K to last 3 sts, k3 tog. Cast off. With right side facing, rejoin yarn to rem sts, k3 tog, k to end. Cast off.

FRONT BODY
Work as given for Back Body to **. Work 38 rows in st st.
Shape Neck
Next row P12, cast off next 7 sts, p to end. Work on last set of sts only. Dec one st at neck edge on next 3 rows. Cast off. With right side facing, rejoin yarn to rem sts and complete as first side.

HEAD (make 2)
With A, cast on 14 sts. P 1 row.
Next row K1, m1, k12, m1, k1. 16 sts.
Beg with a p row, work 7 rows in st st. Dec one st at each end of next row and every alt row until 8 sts rem, ending with a p row. Cast off.

HAIR (make 8)
With B, cast on 11 sts.
Next row K1, [p1, k1] to end.
This row forms moss st patt. Cont in patt until work measures 5cm/2in. Dec one st at each end of next row and foll alt row. Now inc one st at each end of next row and foll alt row. Work a further 5cm/2in. Cast off.

TO MAKE UP
Join shoulder seams of body. Sew in arms, then join side seams. Insert top of legs at lower edge and sew them in place. Stuff body. Leaving cast on edge free, join head pieces together, stuff, then sew in place. With Brown or White, embroider eyes.

Dress

SKIRT
With A, cast on 83 sts. K 3 rows.
Work in patt as follows:
1st row (right side) With A, k.
2nd row With A, p.
3rd row With B, k1, [sl 1, k1] to end.
4th row With B, k1, [yf, sl 1, yb, k1] to end.
5th and 6th rows As 1st and 2nd rows.
7th row With B, k2, [sl 1, k1] to last st, k1.
8th row With B, k2, [yf, sl 1, yb, k1] to last st, k1.
These 8 rows form patt. Cont in patt until work measures 17cm/6¾in from beg, ending with a 2nd row of patt.
Next row K2, [k2 tog] to last st, k1.
Cast off. Make one more piece.

BODICE FRONT
With A, cast on 47 sts. Work 38 rows in patt as given for Skirt.
Shape Neck
Next row Patt 18, turn.
Work on this set of sts only. Dec one st at neck edge on next 5 rows. 13 sts. Patt 6 rows. Cast off.
With right side facing, rejoin yarn to rem sts, cast off centre 11 sts, patt to end. Complete as given for first side.

BODICE RIGHT BACK
With A, cast on 23 sts. Work 39 rows in patt as given for Skirt.
Shape Neck
Cast off 3 sts at beg of next row. Dec one st at neck edge on next 7 rows. 13 sts. Patt 3 rows. Cast off.

BODICE LEFT BACK
Work as given for Bodice Right Back, reversing neck shaping.

SLEEVES
Begin at top edge. With A, cast on 47 sts. Work 30 rows in patt as given for Skirt. Cont in A only.
Next row K1, [k2 tog] to end.
Next row K1, [k twice in next st] to end.
K 2 rows. Cast off.

COLLAR
Using two strands of B together, cast on 28 sts. K 3 rows.
Next row (right side) K.
Next row K2, p24, k2.
Rep last 2 rows 6 times more.
Shape Neck
Next row Patt 10, turn.
Work on this set of sts only. Dec one st at inside edge on next row and foll alt row. 8 sts. Patt 7 rows.
Next row Cast on 6 sts, k2, p to last 2 sts, k2. 14 sts.
Next row K.
Next row K2, p10, k2.
Rep last 2 rows 7 times more. K 4 rows. Cast off. With right side facing, rejoin yarn to rem sts, cast off centre 8 sts, patt to end. Dec one st at inside edge on next row and foll alt row. 8 sts. Patt 8 rows.
Next row Cast on 6 sts, k to end. 14 sts.
Next row K2, p10, k2.
Next row K. Rep last 2 rows 7 times more. K 3 rows. Cast off.

TO MAKE UP
Join shoulder seams. Sew on sleeves, placing centre of sleeves to shoulder seams. Join side and sleeve seams. With crochet hook and A, work 1 row of chain st along back opening and round neck edge, making buttonhole loop at top of left back opening. Sew on button. Join side seams of skirt. Sew skirt to bodice. Make a buttonhole loop at top of left back side of collar opening and sew button to other side.

Ballerina Rabbit

See Page
28

MATERIALS
Rabbit 1 × 50g ball of Rowan Designer DK Wool.
Oddment of Brown yarn for embroidery.
Pair of 3¼mm (No 10/US 3) knitting needles.
Stuffing.
Wrap-over Cardigan and Shoes
1 × 25g hank of Rowan 4 ply Botany.
Pair of 2¾mm (No 12/US 1) knitting needles.
Medium size crochet hook.
Tutu Approximately 15cm/6in of 110cm/43in wide net fabric.
Shirring elastic.

MEASUREMENTS
Rabbit Approximately 20cm/8in high.
Wrap-over Cardigan Actual chest measurement 16cm/6¼in
Length 5.5cm/2¼in
Sleeve seam 4cm/1½in

TENSION
28 sts and 36 rows to 10cm/4in square over st st using DK yarn.
34 sts and 46 rows to 10cm/4in square over st st using 4 ply yarn.

ABBREVIATIONS
See page 10.

Rabbit

Work as given for Small Rabbit with Sweater (see page 46), making legs longer by working 15 rows in st st instead of 9 before shaping top of legs and using Brown to embroider face features.

Wrap-over Cardigan

BACK AND FRONTS
Cast on 28 sts. K 5 rows. Beg with a k row, work 6 rows in st st. Mark each end of last row. Work a further 14 rows.
Shape Neck
Next row K9, cast off next 10 sts, k to end.

Work on last set of sts only for Left Front.
Work 2 rows.
Next row P to last 2 sts, k2.
Next row K2, m1, k to end.
Next row P to last 2 sts, m1, k2.
Rep last 2 rows 5 times more, then work first of the 2 rows again. Mark side edge of last row. Cont inc at front edge as before until there 28 sts. K 4 rows.
Cast off.
With wrong side facing, rejoin yarn to rem sts for Right Front, work 2 rows.
Next row K2, p to end.
Next row K to last 2 sts, m1, k2.
Next row K2, m1, k to end.
Complete as given for first side.

SLEEVES
With right side facing, pick up and k28 sts between markers. Beg with a p row, work 15 rows in st st, dec one st at each

end of every 4th row. 22 sts.
Next row K10, k2 tog, k10.
K 4 rows. Cast off.

TIES (make 2)
Cast on 25 sts. K 2 rows. Cast off.

TO MAKE UP
Join side and sleeve seams. Attach one end of tie at lower front edge of each front. Tie other ends at back.

Shoes

Using 2 strands of yarn together, cast on 12 sts. P 1 row.
Next row K1, [m1, k1] to end.
P 1 row.
Next row K1, m1, k8, [m1, k1] 6 times, k7, m1, k1. 31 sts.
Work 3 rows in st st.
Next row K13, k2 tog, k1, skpo, k13.
P 1 row.
Next row K12, k2 tog, k1, skpo, k12.
P 1 row. Cast off.
Join sole and back seam. With crochet hook, make two 10cm/4in long chain cords for ties. Attach one end of each cord to either side of shoe, then cross other ends over, wrap around leg, secure ends at back of leg. Make one more.

Tutu

Fold net fabric in half widthwise and gather folded edge with length of shirring elastic to fit waist of Rabbit. Tie ends of elastic together.

Fairytale Mice

See Page
29

MATERIALS
For the pair: 1 × 25g balls of Rowan Lightweight DK in each of Grey (A), Cream (B), Green (C) and Purple (D). Small amounts of same in each of Light Pink (E), Dark Pink (F), Red (G) and Black (H).
Pair each of 2¾mm (No 12/US 1) and 3¼mm (No 10/US 3) knitting needles. Stuffing. Small piece of cardboard and glue.

MEASUREMENTS
Mouse Approximately 15cm/6in high.
Shirt or blouse Actual chest measurement 10cm/4in
Length 5cm/2in
Sleeve seam 2cm/¾in
Trousers Actual hip measurement 13cm/5in
Length 6cm/2¼in
Inside leg seam 2.5cm/1in

TENSION
32 sts and 40 rows to 10cm/4in square over st st on 2¾mm (No 12/US 1) needles.
28 sts and 36 rows to 10cm/4in square over st st on 3¼mm (No 10/US 3) needles.

ABBREVIATIONS
See page 10.

Mouse

LEGS (make 2)
Begin at top.
With 2¾mm (No 12/US 1) needles and A, cast on 5 sts. P 1 row.
Next row K twice in each st. 10 sts.
Beg with a p row, work 17 rows in st st.
Next row K1, [k2 tog, k1] to end.
P 1 row.
Next row P1, [p2 tog] to end.
Break off yarn, thread end through rem sts, pull up and secure. Join seam, stuffing leg as you sew.

BODY
Begin at neck edge.
With 2¾mm (No 12/US 1) needles and A, cast on 9 sts. P 1 row.
Next row [K twice in next st] 4 times, k three times in next st, [k twice in next st] 4 times. 19 sts. P 1 row.
Next row K5, m1, k1, m1, k8, m1, k1, m1, k4. P 1 row.
Next row K6, m1, k1, m1, [k5, m1] twice, k1, m1, k5. P 1 row.
Next row K14, m1, k1, m1, k13. 30 sts.
Work 9 rows in st st.
Next row K5, k2 tog, k1, skpo, k3, skpo, k1, k2 tog, k3, k2 tog, k1, skpo, k4.
P 1 row.
Next row K4, k2 tog, k1, skpo, k2, skpo, k3, k2 tog, k1, skpo, k3.
P 1 row.
Next row K3, k2 tog, k1, skpo, k4, k2 tog, k1, skpo, k2. 15 sts.
P 1 row. Cast off.
Join back seam, then cast off edge. Stuff. Gather neck edge, pull up and secure.

ARMS (make 2)
With 2¾mm (No 12/US 1) needles and A, cast on 4 sts. P 1 row.
Next row K1, [m1, k1] to end. 7 sts.
Beg with a p row, work 15 rows in st st.

Next row K1, [k2 tog] to end.
Break off yarn, thread end through rem sts, pull up and secure. Join seam, stuffing arm as you sew.

HEAD
With 2¾mm (No 12/US 1) needles and A, cast on 4 sts. P 1 row.
Next row K1, [m1, k1] to end. P 1 row.
Next row K1, [m1, k2, m1, k1] to end.
Work 3 rows in st st.
Next row K1, [m1, k3] 3 times, m1, k1.
P 1 row.
Next row K1, m1, k to last st, m1, k1.
Next row P1, m1, p to last st, m1, p1.
Next row K1, [m1, k3] twice, m1, k5, [m1, k3] twice, m1, k1. 25 sts.
Mark each end of last row. Work 6 rows.
Next row P4, p2 tog, p13, p2 tog tbl, p4.
Next row K14, skpo, turn.
Next row Sl 1, p5, p2 tog, turn.
Next row Sl 1, k5, skpo, turn.
Rep last 2 rows 6 times more.
Cast off purlwise working last 2 sts tog.
Join seam from point to markers and stuff head.

OUTER EARS (make 2)
With 2¾mm (No 12/US 1) needles and A, cast on 7 sts. Beg with a k row, work 4 rows in st st.
Next row Skpo, k3, k2 tog. P 1 row.
Next row Skpo, k1, k2 tog.
P3 tog and fasten off.

INNER EARS (make 2)
With 2¾mm (No 12/US 1) needles and E, cast on 6 sts. Beg with a k row, work 3 rows in st st.
Next row P2 tog, p2, p2 tog tbl.
Next row Skpo, k2 tog.
P2 tog and fasten off.

TAIL
With 2¾mm (No 12/US 1) needles and A,

cast on 25 sts. Cast off.

TO MAKE UP
Sew head to body. Attach yarn at seam just below top of one arm, thread through body at shoulder position, then attach other arm, pull up yarn tightly and thread through body again in same place, attach yarn to first arm again and fasten off. Attach legs at lower edge of body in same way as arms. With right sides of inner and outer ears together, join seam all round, leaving cast on edge free. Turn to right side and close opening. Fold this edge in half and secure, then sew in place. With Black, embroider face features and whiskers. Attach tail.

Shirt

BACK AND FRONT
With 3¼mm (No 10/US 3) needles and B, cast on 14 sts. K 3 rows. Beg with a k row, work 8 rows in st st. Mark each end of last row. Work a further 6 rows.
Shape Neck
Next row K5, turn.
Work 4 rows on this set of sts only.
Next row Cast on 2, k2, p5. K 1 row.
Next row K2, p5. K 1 row.
Mark beg of last row. Rep last 2 rows once. Leave these sts on a holder.
Rejoin yarn at inside edge to rem sts, cast off next 4 sts, k to end. Work 3 rows.
Next row Cast on 2, k to end.
Next row P5, k2. K 1 row.
Rep last 2 rows once. Mark end of last row. Work a further 2 rows.
Next row P to end, then p across sts on holder.
Work 5 rows. K 3 rows. Cast off.

SLEEVES
With 3¼mm (No 10/US 3) needles, right side facing and B, pick up and k12 sts between markers. Beg with a p row, work 6 rows in st st. K 3 rows. Cast off.

TO MAKE UP
Join side and sleeve seams.

Blouse

BACK AND FRONT
Work as given for Back and Front of Shirt.

SLEEVES
Work as given for Sleeves of Shirt.

COLLAR
With 3¼mm (No 10/US 3) needles, right side facing and B, pick up and k23 sts around neck edge. P 1 row.
Next row [K twice in next st] to end.
46 sts. K 4 rows.

Next row K1, m1, k44, m1, k1.
Cast off knitwise.

TO MAKE UP
Join side and sleeve seams.

Trousers

BACK AND FRONT ALIKE
With 3¼mm (No 10/US 3) needles and C,
cast on 18 sts. K 3 rows. Beg with a k
row, work 14 rows in st st.
Next row K7, k2 tog, turn.
Work 3 rows on this set of sts only. K 3
rows. Cast off.
With right side facing, rejoin yarn to rem
sts, k2 tog, k to end. Work 3 rows. K 3
rows. Cast off.

STRAPS (make 2)
With 3¼mm (No 10/US 3) needles and D,
cast on 18 sts. K 1 row. Cast off.

TO MAKE UP
Join side and inside leg seams. Sew
straps in place. With G, embroider buttons. When on, pull tail through stitches.

Skirt

With 3¼mm (No 10/US 3) needles and D,
cast on 60 sts. K 5 rows.
Next row K to end.
Next row K3, p54, k3.
Rep last 2 rows 4 times more.
Next row K3, [k2 tog] to last 3 sts, k3.
33 sts. K 3 rows.
Next row Cast on 20 sts for tie, cast off to
last st, cast on 20 sts, cast off.
With 3¼mm (No 10/US 3) needles and C,
cast on 18 sts for strap. K 1 row. Cast off.
Make one more.
With 3¼mm (No 10/US 3) needles and
C, cast on 10 sts for horizontal strap.
Cast off.
Sew straps in place. With G, work 1 row
of cross stitches around hem of skirt and
embroider buttons.

Pants

With 3¼mm (No 10/US 3) needles and B,
cast on 14 sts. K 3 rows. Beg with a k
row, work 14 rows in st st.
Shape Leg
Dec one st at each end of next row and foll
alt row. 10 sts. P 1 row. K 3 rows.
Cast off. Make one more. Join leg seams,

then front and back seams, leaving small
opening at back seam for tail.

Shoes

SOLE
With 2¾mm (No 12/US 1) needles and H
or A, cast on 3 sts. P 1 row.
Next row K1, [m1, k1] twice.
Next row P1, m1, p3, m1, p1. 7 sts.
Beg with a k row, work 4 rows in st st.
Next row Skpo, k3, k2 tog. P 1 row.
Next row Skpo, k1, k2 tog.
P3 tog and fasten off.

UPPER
With 2¾mm (No 12/US 1) needles and G
or F, cast on 12 sts. K 2 rows.
Next row K1, m1, k to last st, m1, k1.
K 1 row.
Rep last 2 rows 4 times. 22 sts. K 2 rows.
Cast off.

TO MAKE UP
Glue soles to piece of cardboard. When
dry, cut out soles. Sew cast off edge of
uppers to soles, then join front seams,
leaving top 3 rows free. With H, lace
shoes.

Tartan Bear

See Page
31

MATERIALS
2 × 25g hanks of Rowan Lightweight DK
in Red.
1 × 25g hank of same in each of Navy,
Green and Yellow.
Pair of 3¼mm (No 10/US 3) knitting needles.
2 buttons.
Stuffing.

MEASUREMENTS
Approximately 23cm/9in high.

TENSION
28 sts and 36 rows to 10cm/4in square
over st st.

ABBREVIATIONS
See page 10.

NOTES
Read chart from right to left on right
side (k) rows and from left to right on
wrong side (p) rows. When working in
pattern, use separate lengths of
contrast yarns for each coloured area
and twist yarns together on wrong side
at joins to avoid holes.

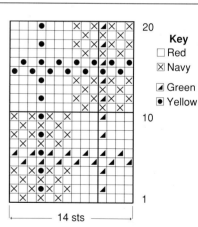

Key
□ Red
☒ Navy
◪ Green
◉ Yellow

14 sts

LEGS (make 2)
With Red, cast on 35 sts. Beg with a k
row, work in st st and patt from chart as
follows:
1st row Work 14 sts of 1st row of chart
twice, then work first 7 sts.
2nd row Work last 7 sts of 2nd row of
chart, then rep 14 sts twice.
Work a further 8 rows as set.
Next row Patt 10, cast off next 14 sts,
patt to end.
Work a further 19 rows in patt across all
sts. Cast off.

SOLES (make 2)

With Red, cast on 14 sts. Beg with a k
row, work in st st and patt from chart for
10 rows. Cast off.

BODY (make 2)
With Red, cast on 28 sts. Beg with a k
row, work in st st and patt from chart for
30 rows. Cast off.

ARMS (make 2)
With Red, cast on 21 sts. Beg with a k
row, work in st st and patt from chart as
follows:
1st row Work 14 sts of 1st row of chart
then work first 7 sts.

2nd row Work last 7 sts of 2nd row of
chart, then work 14 sts.
Work a further 24 rows as set. Cast off.

HEAD (make 2)
Work as given for Arms.

EARS (make 2)
Work as given for Soles.

TO MAKE UP
Join instep seam of legs. Rounding seam
at top corners, join top and back leg
seam, leaving an opening. Sew in soles
tapering corners. Stuff and close

opening. Make darts at centre of cast on and cast off edges of each body piece, making top darts longer. With right sides together, join body pieces together, tapering corners and leaving top edge open. Turn to right side and stuff firmly. Gather top edge, pull up and secure. Fold arms lengthwise and rounding seam at top and lower edge corners, join seams, leaving an opening. Stuff firmly

and close opening. With right sides of head pieces together and leaving cast on edge free, sew around edges, tapering corners at back edge and forming point at centre of front edge for nose. Turn to right side and stuff firmly. Gather open edge, pull up and secure. Sew head in place. Attach yarn 1cm/¼in below top at centre of one arm, thread through body at shoulder position, attach other arm, then thread

yarn through body in same place again, pull up tightly, attach yarn to first arm again and fasten off. Attach legs at lower edge of body in same way as arms. With right sides of paired ear pieces together, work seam around, tapering corners and leaving cast on edge free. Turn to right side and close opening. Make a "dimple" in centre of each ear. Sew them in place. Sew on buttons in place for eyes.

Teddy Bear with Fair Isle Slipover

See Page
30

MATERIALS
Teddy Bear 2×25g hanks of Rowan 4 ply Botany in Brown (A) and small amount in Black (B).
Pair of 2¾mm (No 12/US 1) knitting needles.
Stuffing.
Slipover 1×25g hank of Rowan Lightweight DK in each of Navy (A) and Beige.
Small amount of same in each of Dark Red, Gold and Green.
Pair of 3¾mm (No 9/US 4) knitting needles.

MEASUREMENTS
Teddy Bear Approximately 32cm/12½in high.
Slipover Actual chest measurement 27cm/10½in
Length 11cm/4¼in

TENSION
34 sts and 46 rows to 10cm/4in square over st st using 4 ply yarn and 2¾mm (No 12/US 1) needles.
26 sts and 30 rows to 10cm/4in square over coloured pattern using DK yarn and 3¾mm (No 9/US 4) needles.

ABBREVIATIONS
See page 10.

NOTE
When working in coloured pattern, read chart from right to left on right side (k) rows and from left to right on wrong side (p) rows.

Edge sts | ← Rep 10 sts →

KEY
☐ Navy (A)
• Beige
☒ Dark Red
◪ Gold
◉ Green

Teddy Bear

Work as given for Teddy Bear with Smock (see page 55).

Slipover

BACK
With A, cast on 35 sts.
1st row (right side) K1, [p1, k1] to end.
2nd row P1, [k1, p1] to end.
Beg with a k row, work 2 rows in st st.
Cont in st st and patt from chart, work 12 rows.
Shape Armholes
Keeping patt correct, cast off 5 sts at beg of next 2 rows. Dec one st at each end of next 3 rows. 19 sts. ** Work a further 9 rows in patt.
Cont in A only, work 1 row.

Shape Neck
Next row P5, cast off next 9 sts, p to end.
Work on last set of 5 sts only for 3 rows.
Leave these sts on a safety pin.
With right side facing, rejoin yarn to rem sts for second side and work 3 rows.
Leave these sts on a safety pin.

FRONT
Work as given for Back to **
Shape Neck
Next row Patt 9, turn.
Work on this set of sts only. Dec one st at neck edge on foll 4 rows.
Patt 4 rows. Cont in A only, work 4 rows.
Leave these sts on a safety pin.
With wrong side facing, slip centre st onto a safety pin, rejoin yarn to rem sts and patt to end. Complete to match first side.

NECKBAND
Graft right shoulder sts together.
With right side facing and A, pick up and k10 sts down left front neck, k st from safety pin, pick up and k10 sts up right front neck, 6 sts down right back neck, 8 sts from centre back neck and 6 sts up left back neck. 41 sts. Work 3 rows in rib as given for Back welt, dec one st at each side of centre st on front on last 2 rows. Cast off in rib.

ARMBANDS
With right side facing and A, pick up and k41 sts evenly around armhole edge. Work 2 rows in rib as given for Back welt. Cast off in rib.

TO MAKE UP
Place slipover on Teddy and graft left shoulder sts together, then join neckband seam. Join side and armbands seams.

Angel Rabbit

See Page
32

MATERIALS
Rabbit 1×25g hank of Rowan 4 ply Botany.
Oddment of Black yarn for embroidery.
Pair of 2¾mm (No 12/US 1) knitting needles.
Stuffing.
Smock 1×50g ball of Rowan Cotton Glace.
Length of Gold lurex yarn.
Pair of 3¼mm (No 10/US 3) knitting needles.
Wings Approximately 25cm×20cm/10in×8in piece of gold thick card. 13cm/5in of gold wire.

MEASUREMENTS
Rabbit Approximately 17cm/6½in high.
Smock Actual chest measurement 14cm/5½in
Length 10cm/4in
Sleeve seam 5cm/2in

TENSION
34 sts and 46 rows to 10cm/4in square over st st using 4 ply yarn.
26 sts and 32 rows to 10cm/4in square over st st using cotton yarn.

ABBREVIATIONS
See page 10.

Rabbit

LEGS (make 2)
Cast on 12 sts. P 1 row.
Next row K1, [m1, k1] to end.
P 1 row.
Next row K1, m1, k8, [m1, k1] 6 times, k7, m1, k1. 31 sts.
Work 3 rows in st st.
Next row K13, k2 tog, k1, skpo, k13.
P 1 row.
Next row K12, k2 tog, k1, skpo, k12. 27 sts. P 1 row.
Next row K7, cast off next 13 sts, k to end.
Work 19 rows in st st across all sts, inc one st at each end of 2nd row. 16 sts.
Next row K1, k2 tog, k1, skpo, k3, k2 tog, k1, skpo, k2.
P 1 row.
Next row K2 tog, k1, skpo, k1, k2 tog, k1, skpo, k1.
Next row [P2 tog] to end.
Break off yarn, thread end through rem sts, pull up and secure. Join instep seam, then sole and back leg seam, leaving an opening. Stuff and close opening.

BODY
Begin at neck edge.
Cast on 15 sts. P 1 row.
Next row K1, [m1, k1] to end. 29 sts.
Beg with a p row, work 5 rows in st st.
Next row [K7, m1] twice, k1, [m1, k7] twice.
Work 3 rows.
Next row K16, m1, k1, m1, k16. 35 sts.

Work 13 rows.
Next row K15, skpo, k1, k2 tog, k15.
Work 3 rows.
Next row K14, skpo, k1, k2 tog, k14.
Work 3 rows.
Next row K1, [k2 tog] to end. 16 sts.
P 1 row. Cast off.

ARMS (make 2)
Cast on 6 sts. P 1 row.
Next row K1, [m1, k1] to end.
P 1 row.
Next row K1, [m1, k4, m1, k1] twice. 15 sts. Work 11 rows.
Next row K1, [skpo, k2, k2 tog, k1] twice.
Work 3 rows. Inc one st at each end of next row. 13 sts. Work 15 rows.
Next row K1, [skpo, k1, k2 tog, k1] twice.
P 1 row.
Next row K1, [k2 tog] to end.
Break off yarn, thread end through rem sts, pull up and secure. Join underarm seam, leaving an opening. Stuff and close opening.

HEAD
Begin at back.
Cast on 7 sts. P 1 row.
Next row K1, [m1, k1] to end.
Rep last 2 rows once more. 25 sts. Work 5 rows.
Next row K1, [m1, k3] to end. 33 sts.
Work 15 rows.
Next row K1, [k2 tog] to end.
Work 5 rows.
Next row K1, [k2 tog] to end. 9 sts.
P 1 row. Break off yarn, thread end through rem sts, pull up and secure. Join seam, leaving an opening. Stuff and close opening.

EARS (make 2)
Cast on 14 sts. K 24 rows.
Next row Skpo, k to last 2 sts, k2 tog.
K 2 rows.
Rep last 3 rows until 2 sts rem. K2 tog and fasten off.

TO MAKE UP
Fold sides of body to centre, then join together cast off edge. Gather neck edge of body, pull up and secure. Join back seam, leaving an opening. Stuff and close opening. Sew head in position. Fold cast on edges of ears in half and sew them in place. With Black, embroider nose, mouth and eyes. Attach yarn at seam about 1cm/¼in below top of one arm, thread yarn through body at shoulder position, then attach other arm, pull yarn tightly and thread through body again in same place, attach yarn to first arm again and fasten off. Attach legs at lower edge of body in same way as arms.

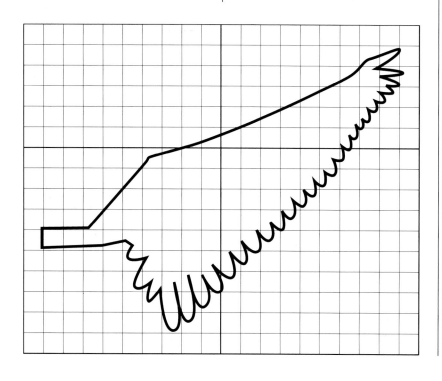

Smock

BACK AND FRONT
Begin at back hem.
Cast on 26 sts. K 3 rows. Beg with a k row, work 22 rows in st st. Mark each end of last row.
Next row K5, [k2 tog] 8 times, k5. 18 sts.
P 1 row.
Shape Neck
Next row K7, k2 tog, turn.
Work on this set of sts only for first side of neck. Dec one st at neck edge on 2 foll alt rows. 6 sts. Work 2 rows. Leave these sts.
Rejoin yarn at inside edge to rem sts for

second side of neck and k2 tog, k to end.
Dec one st at neck edge on 2 foll alt rows. Work 2 rows.
Next row P to end, cast on 6 sts, then p across sts of first side.
Work 6 rows.
Next row K5, [m1, k1] 8 times, k5. 26 sts.
Mark each end of last row. Work 22 rows in st st. K 2 rows. Cast off.

SLEEVES
With right side facing, pick up and k20 sts between markers. P 1 row.
Next row K6, [k twice in next st] 8 times, k6. 28 sts.

Work 12 rows in st st. K 2 rows. Cast off.

TO MAKE UP
Join side and sleeve seams. Dress Rabbit in smock. Wind lurex yarn around neck, crossing over chest and then around chest, tying at back.

Wings

Trace diagram of wing, transfer onto gold card, making it into a pair joined at centre. Cut out wings. Make a circle for halo at one end of wire. Attach other end at centre of wings. Sew them in place.

Skating Elephant

See Page
33

MATERIALS
1×50g ball of Rowan Designer DK Wool in Dark Grey (A).
Small amount of same in each of Cream (B), Red (C), Light Green (D) and Black (E).
Length of Silver lurex DK yarn.
Pair of 2¾mm (No 12/US 1) and 3¼ mm (No 10/US 3) knitting needles.
Approximately 8cm × 4cm/3in × 15¾in piece of fabric.
2 plastic press studs and safety pin.
Stuffing and pipe cleaner.
Small piece of cardboard and glue.

MEASUREMENTS
Elephant Approximately 18cm/7in high.
Sweater Actual chest measurement 14cm/5½in
Length 6cm/2¼in
Sleeve seam 3cm/1¼in

TENSION
28 sts and 36 rows to 10cm/4in square over st st on 3¼mm (No 10/US 3) needles.

ABBREVIATIONS
See page 10.

Elephant

LEGS (make 2)
With 3¼mm (No 10/US 3) needles and A, cast on 12 sts. P 1 row.
Next row K1, [m1, k1] to end. 23 sts.
Beg with a p row, work 3 rows in st st.
Next row K9, skpo, k1, k2 tog, k9.
Work 3 rows.
Next row K8, skpo, k1, k2 tog, k8. 19 sts.
Work 9 rows.
Next row K2, k2 tog, k2, skpo, k3, k2 tog, k2, skpo, k2.
P 1 row.

Next row K1, [k2 tog] to end.
Break off yarn, thread end through rem sts, pull up and secure. Gather cast on edge, pull up and secure. Join inner leg seam, leaving an opening. Stuff firmly and close opening.

BODY
Begin at neck edge.
With 3¼mm (No 10/US 3) needles and A, cast on 15 sts. P 1 row.
Next row K1, [m1, k1] to end. 29 sts.
Beg with a p row, work 5 rows in st st.
Next row [K7, m1] twice, k1, [m1, k7] twice.
Work 3 rows.
Next row K16, m1, k1, m1, k16. 35 sts.
Work 5 rows.
Next row K15, skpo, k1, k2 tog, k15.
Work 3 rows.
Next row K14, skpo, k1, k2 tog, k14.
Work 3 rows.
Next row K1, [k2 tog] to end. 16 sts.
P 1 row. Cast off.

ARMS (make 2)
Work as given for Legs.

HEAD
Begin at back.
With 3¼mm (No 10/US 3) needles and A, cast on 7 sts. P 1 row.
Next row K1, [m1, k1] to end.
Rep last 2 rows once more. 25 sts.
Work 3 rows in st st.
Next row K1, [m1, k3] to end. 33 sts.
Work 11 rows.
Next row K1, [k2 tog] to end.
Work 5 rows.
Next row K2 tog, [k3, k2 tog] to end. 13 sts. Work 5 rows.
Next row K1, skpo, k7, k2 tog, k1.
Work 3 rows.
Next row K1, skpo, k5, k2 tog, k1.
Work 11 rows.
Next row K1, [k2 tog] to end.
P 1 row. Break off yarn, thread end through rem sts, pull up and secure.
Join seam, leaving an opening. Insert

pipe cleaner into trunk, then stuff trunk and head. Close opening. Bend trunk into desired shape.

EARS (make 2)
With 3¼mm (No 10/US 3) needles and A, cast on 16 sts. K 10 rows.
Next row K1, skpo, k to last 3 sts, k2 tog, k1.
K 1 row. Rep last 2 rows once more. Cast off.

TO MAKE UP
Fold sides of body to centre, then join cast off edge. Gather neck edge of body, pull up and secure. Join back seam, leaving an opening. Stuff firmly and close opening. Sew head in position. Gather cast on edge of ears slightly and sew them in place. With Black, embroider eyes and mouth. Attach yarn at seam about 1cm/¼in below top of one arm, thread yarn through body at shoulder position, then attach other arm, pull yarn tightly and thread through body again in same place, then attach yarn to first arm again and fasten off. Attach legs at lower edge of body in same way as arms.

Sweater

BACK AND FRONT ALIKE
With 3¼mm (No 10/US 3) needles and B, cast on 20 sts. Beg with a p row, work 3 rows in st st. Work 4 rows in k2, p2 rib.
Beg with a k row, work 4 rows in st st. Mark each end of last row. Work a further 3 rows. K 2 rows.
Next row [P1, k1] to end.
Next row [K1, p1] to end.
Rep last 2 rows 3 times.
Shape Shoulders
Cast off 5 sts at beg of next 2 rows. 10 sts. Work 2 rows in k1, p1 rib, inc one st at each end of every row. 14 sts. Rib 1 row. Beg with a k row, work 3 rows in st st. Cast off.

SLEEVES

With right side facing, 3¼mm (No 10/US 3) needles and B, pick up and k10 sts along side edge of one piece from marker to shoulder and 10 sts from shoulder to marker of second piece. 20 sts. Work 3 rows in k2, p2 rib. Beg with a k row, work 4 rows in st st. Now work 2 rows in k2, p2 rib. Cast off in rib.

TO MAKE UP

Join side and sleeve seams. Dress Elephant, then join shoulder and neckband seams.

Kilt

Cut off strip approximately 1.5cm/½in wide along longer edge of fabric for waist band. Turn hems at lower edge and along shorter edges of larger piece to wrong side and stitch in place. Leaving first 4cm/1½in straight, gather remainder of top edge to fit elephants waist. Cut strip for waist band to fit top of skirt, fold in half and sew in place. Sew on press studs. Pin safety pin in place.

Scarf

With 3¼mm (No 10/US 3) needles and C, cast on 10 sts.
1st row K2, [p2, k2] to end.
2nd row P2, [k2, p2] to end.
Rep last 2 rows until scarf measures 25cm/10in. Cast off in rib.

Hat

With 3¼mm (No 10/US 3) needles and C, cast on 22 sts.
1st row K2, [p2, k2] to end.
2nd row P2, [k2, p2] to end.
Rep last 2 rows twice more.
Next row K2, [p2 tog, k2] to end.
Next row P2, [k1, p2] to end.
Break off yarn, thread end through rem sts, pull up and join seam, reversing seam on last 2 rows for brim. Turn back brim. Make a small pompon in C and attach to top of hat. Sew hat to head.

Skating Boots

SOLE

With 2¾mm (No 12/US 1) needles and E, cast on 3 sts. P 1 row.
Next row K1, [m1, k1] twice.
Next row P1, m1, p3, m1, p1. 7 sts.
Beg with a k row, work 4 rows in st st.
Next row Skpo, k3, k2 tog.
P 1 row.
Next row Skpo, k1, k2 tog.
P3 tog and fasten off.

UPPER

With 2¾mm (No 12/US 1) needles and D, cast on 22 sts. K 2 rows.
Next row Skpo, k to last 2 sts, k2 tog.
K 1 row. Rep last 2 rows 4 times more. 12 sts. Cast off.

BLADE

With 2¾mm (No 12/US 1) needles and lurex yarn, cast on 12 sts. Cast off.

TO MAKE UP

Glue soles to piece of cardboard. Cut out soles when dry. Sew cast on edge of uppers to soles. Join front seams. Attach blades loosely in 2 places to soles of boots. With E, lace shoes, leaving long ends. Tie ends together and place round Elephant's neck.

Dalmatian Dog

See Page
35

MATERIALS

3 × 25g hanks of Rowan Lightweight DK in Cream (A) and 1 hank in Black.
Oddment of Dark Brown yarn for embroidery.
Pair of 3¼mm (No 10/US 3) knitting needles.
Small piece of Red felt.
Stuffing.

MEASUREMENTS

Approximately 20cm/8in high and 20cm/8in long.

TENSION

28 sts and 36 rows to 10cm/4in square over st st.

ABBREVIATIONS

See page 10.

NOTE

When working coloured pattern from charts, use separate lengths of Black yarn for each spot and twist yarns together on wrong side at joins to avoid holes.

LEFT OUTER BACK LEG

With A, cast on 32 sts. Mark 1st and 10th sts from beg. Beg with a k row, work in st st and patt from Back Leg chart, reading k rows from right to left and p rows from left to right, work 11 rows. Cast off 17 sts at beg of next row. 15 sts. Work 8 rows straight. Cast off 4 sts at beg of next row and foll alt row. P 1 row. Cast off rem 7 sts.

LEFT INNER BACK LEG

Work as given for Left Outer Back Leg, using A throughout and reversing shaping by reading p for k and k for p.

RIGHT OUTER BACK LEG

Work as given for Left Outer Back Leg, reversing shaping and patt from chart by reading p for k and k for p.

RIGHT INNER BACK LEG

Work as given for Left Outer Back Leg, using A throughout.

LEFT OUTSIDE BODY

Front Leg
With A, cast on 12 sts. Beg with a k row, work in st st and patt from Body chart for Leg, reading chart from right to left on k rows and from left to right on p rows, work 1 row. Cont working from chart, inc one st at end of next row and at beg of foll row. 14 sts. Work 3 rows straight. Dec one st at end of next row. Cast off 4 sts at beg of foll row. 9 sts. Work 14 rows straight. Inc one st at end of next row and foll 6th row. 11 sts. Work 5 rows straight. Leave these sts on a holder.
Back
With A, cast on 7 sts. Beg with a k row, work in st st and patt from Body chart for Back, reading chart from right to left on k rows and from left to right on p rows, work 1 row. Cont working from chart, cast on 4 sts at beg of next row and foll alt row, then 2 sts at beg of foll alt row. Inc one st at end of next row and at same edge on foll 2 rows, then on foll alt row. 21 sts. Work 3 rows straight. Dec one st at beg of next row. Work 1 row. Dec one st at end of next row and foll 4th row. Work 3 rows. Dec one st at beg of next row. Work 2 rows. Inc one st at beg of next row and foll alt row, then one st at same edge on foll 4th row. 23 sts.
Next row K2 tog, patt 21, cast on 4 sts, then patt across leg sts. 37 sts.
Dec one st at beg of 2 foll 4th rows, then foll alt row. Work 1 row. Mark beg of last row. Dec one st at each end of next row and foll alt row.
Next row P to last 2 sts, p2 tog.

Leg Chart

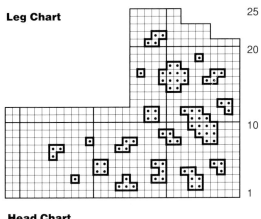

25
20
10
1

Head Chart

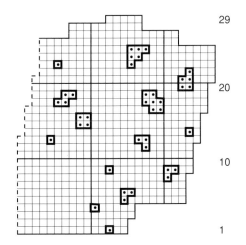

29
20
10
1

Body Chart

64
60
50
40
30
20
10
1

Leg   Back

KEY
☐ Cream (A)
⊡ Black

Ear Chart

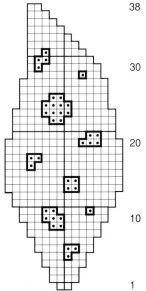

38
30
20
10
1

Next row K2 tog, k to last 2 sts, k2 tog.
Rep last 2 rows twice more, then work first of the 2 rows again.
Next row Cast off 3 sts, k to last 2 sts, k2 tog.
P 1 row. Rep last 2 rows 3 times more. Mark beg of last row. Cast off rem 4 sts.

RIGHT OUTSIDE BODY
Work as given for Left Outside Body, reversing shaping and patt from chart by reading p for k and k for p.

RIGHT INSIDE BODY AND FRONT LEG
With A, cast on 12 sts. Beg with a k row, work in st st, inc one st at end of 2nd row and at beg of foll row. 14 sts. Work 3 rows straight. Dec one st at end of next row. Cast off 4 sts at beg of foll row. 9 sts. Work 14 rows. Inc one st at end of next row and foll 6th row. Work 2 rows. Inc one st at end of next row and at each end of foll alt row. Leave these sts on a spare needle.
With A, cast on 6 sts. Beg with a p row, cont in st st, work 1 row. Cast on 4 sts at beg of next 4 rows. 22 sts.
Next row Cast on 4 sts, k to end, cast on 4 sts, then k across sts on a spare needle. 44 sts.
Cast on 3 sts at beg of next row and 4 sts at beg of foll alt row. Rep last 2 rows once. 58 sts. Cast on 2 sts at beg of next row. Work 1 row. Cast off.

LEFT INSIDE BODY AND FRONT LEG
Work as Right Inside Body and Front Leg, reversing shaping by reading p for k and k for p.

SOLES (make 4)
Begin at back. With A, cast on 4 sts. Work in st st, inc one st at each end of 3rd row and foll alt row. 8 sts. Work 3 rows. Dec one st at each end of next 3 rows. Work 2 tog and fasten off.

HEAD
Begin at front. With A, cast on 3 sts for mouth gusset. Beg with a k row, work in st st, inc one st at each end of 3rd row and foll 4th row, then on foll alt row. 9 sts. Work 3 rows straight. Dec one st at each end of next row and foll 4th row. Work 3 rows. Cast on 10 sts at beg of next 2 rows. 25 sts. Inc one st at each end of next 2 rows. Mark each end of last row. Work 2 rows. Dec one st at each end of next row. Work 3 rows. Inc one st at each end of next row. Work 1 row.
Next row Reading chart from right to left, work 1st row of Head chart inc one st in first st, k1A, reading chart from left to right, work 1st row of Head chart inc one st in last st.
Next row Reading chart from right to left, work 2nd row, p1A, reading chart from left to right, work 2nd row.
Cont working from chart as set, inc one st at each end of next row. Work 1 row. Cast on 7 sts at beg of next 2 rows. 47 sts.

Mark each end of last row. Work 2 rows. Inc one st at each end of next row. Work 3 rows.

Next row Inc in first st, k21, k2 tog, k1, skpo, k21, inc in last st.

Work 3 rows straight. Rep last 4 rows twice more. Mark each end of last row.

Next row Cast off 5 sts, k18 sts more, turn. Work on this set of sts only. Cast off 4 sts at beg of next row and 5 sts at beg of foll 2 rows. Cast off rem 5 sts.

With right side facing, rejoin yarn to rem sts and cast off 5 sts at beg of next 4 rows. Cast off rem 5 sts.

RIGHT OUTER EAR

With A, cast on 2 sts. Beg with a p row, work in st st and patt from Ear chart, reading k rows from right to left and p rows from left to right, work 4 rows inc one st at each end of 2nd and 4th rows. Cont working from chart, inc one st at each end of every alt row until there are 16 sts. Work 5 rows straight. Dec one st at each end of next row and 2 foll 4th rows. Work 1 row straight. Mark end of last row. Dec one st at beg of next row and at same edge on every row until 2 sts rem. Work 2 tog and fasten off.

RIGHT INNER EAR

Work as given for Right Outer Ear, using A throughout and reversing shaping by reading p for k and k for p.

LEFT OUTER EAR

Work as given for Right Outer Ear, reversing shaping and patt from chart by reading p for k and k for p.

LEFT INNER EAR

Work as given for Right Outer Ear, using A throughout.

TO MAKE UP

Join cast off edges of inside body together. Join back and top seam of outside body from cast on edge to markers. Join inside body to outside body placing centre seam of inside body to seam at back of outside body and to markers at top of legs and leaving cast on edges of legs free. Sew in soles. Stuff body firmly. Fold head piece in half and join top seam from markers. Join underchin seam between markers. Sew mouth gusset in place. Stuff head firmly and sew open edge to open edge of body. Join paired back leg pieces together, leaving an opening on top and bottom between markers. Sew in soles. Stuff legs firmly and close opening. Sew legs in place. Join paired ear pieces together and sew edges between marker and top in place. With Black, embroider mouth and "whiskers". Embroider eyes with Brown and Cream yarn. Cut tongue out in Red felt and sew to mouth. Attach length of A yarn at inside edge of back foot, insert needle through centre of front feet, pull up the yarn and attach it at inside edge of second back foot, pull up and fasten off.

Scottie Dog

See Page 34

MATERIALS
1 × 50g ball of Rowan Designer DK Wool.
Pair of 3¼mm (No 10/US 3) knitting needles.
Stuffing.
Length of ribbon.

MEASUREMENTS
Approximately 10cm/4in high and 20cm/8in long.

TENSION
28 sts and 36 rows to 10cm/4in square over st st.

ABBREVIATIONS
See page 10.

UPPER BODY
Back Leg
Cast on 12 sts. Beg with a k row, work 4 rows in st st.

Next row K2 tog, k to last st, k twice in last st. Work 3 rows.

Next row K2 tog, k to last st, k twice in last st.

P 1 row. Leave these sts on a spare needle.

Front Leg
Cast on 12 sts. Beg with a k row, work 10 rows in st st.

Next row K to end, then cast on 8 sts and k across sts of back leg. 32 sts. P 1 row. Inc one st at end of next row. Work 3 rows. ** Mark each end of last row. Dec one st at each end of next row. Dec one st at beg of next row and at end of foll row. Work 3 rows.

Next row K2 tog, k to last st, k twice in last st. 29 sts.

Work 11 rows.

Next row K twice in first st, k to last 2 sts, k2 tog.

Work 3 rows. Inc one st at end of next row and at beg of foll row. Inc one st at each end of next row. Mark each end of last row. *** Work 3 rows. Dec one st at end of next row. 32 sts. Work 1 row.

Next row K12, cast off 8 sts, k to end. Work on last set of sts for back leg. P 1 row.

Next row K twice in first st, k to last 2 sts, k2 tog.

Work 3 rows.

Next row K twice in first st, k to last 2 sts, k2 tog.

Work 4 rows. Cast off.

With wrong side facing, rejoin yarn to rem sts for front leg and work 10 rows. Cast off.

UNDERSIDE
Work as given for Upper Body to **. Work 3 rows, marking each end of 2nd row. Work as given for Upper Body from *** to end.

HEAD SIDES
Begin at neck edge.
Cast on 11 sts for left side. Beg with a k row, work 3 rows in st st.
Cast on 10 sts at beg of next row. 21 sts. Work 12 rows. Dec one st at each end of next row. Cast off.
Work another piece for right side but casting on 10 sts at end of 4th row.

HEAD GUSSET
Cast on 3 sts. Beg with a p row, cont in st st, work 1 row. Inc one st at each end of next row and 2 foll 4th rows. 9 sts. Work 27 rows.
Dec one st at each end of next row and 2 foll 4th rows. 3 sts. P 1 row. Cast off.

EARS (make 4)
Cast on 8 sts. Work 4 rows in st st. Dec one st at each end of next row and 2 foll 3rd rows. Work 2 tog and fasten off.

TAIL (make 2)
Cast on 11 sts. Work 3 rows in st st. Dec one st at each end of next row and 3 foll 4th rows. Work 3 tog and fasten off.

SOLES (make 4)
Cast on 3 sts. P 1 row. Cont in st st, inc one st at each end of next 3 rows. Work 7 rows. Dec one st at each end of next 3 rows. P 1 row. K3 tog and fasten off.

TO MAKE UP
Fold upper body in half and join back seam from folded end to markers.
Join underside to body, matching markers and legs and leaving lower edges of legs open. Sew in soles. Join underchin seam of sides of head.
Sew in head gusset. Stuff body and head firmly. Sew head in place.
Join paired ear pieces together stuffing slightly. Sew ears in place. Place ribbon around neck and tie it into a bow.

Reindeer

See Page
36

MATERIALS
3 × 25g hanks of Rowan Lightweight DK.
Oddments of Black and White yarn for embroidery.
Pair of 3¼mm (No 10/US 3) knitting needles.
Small piece of Brown felt.
Stuffing.

MEASUREMENTS
Approximately 34cm/13½in high and 32cm/12in long.

TENSION
28 sts and 36 rows to 10cm/4in square over st st.

ABBREVIATIONS
See page 10.

UPPER BODY
Cast on 30 sts. Mark centre of cast on row. P 1 row.
Next row Cast on 5 sts, k to end.
Next row Cast on 5 sts, p to end.
Mark each end of last row.
Shape Back Legs
Next row Cast on 5 sts, k24, m1, k2, m1, k19.
Cont in st st, cast on 5 sts at beg of next 3 rows. 62 sts.
Next row Cast on 20 sts, k50, m1, k2, m1, k30.
Cast on 20 sts at beg of next row. 104 sts. Work 2 rows.
Next row K51, m1, k2, m1, k51.
Work 3 rows.
Next row K52, m1, k2, m1, k52.
Work 3 rows.
Next row K53, m1, k2, m1, k53.
Work 1 row.
Next row K8, yf, sl 1, yb, turn, sl 1, p8, turn, k6, yf, sl 1, yb, turn, sl 1, p6, turn, k4, yf, sl 1, yb, turn, sl 1, p4, turn, cast off 27 sts, k to end.
Next row P8, sl 1, yf, turn, sl 1, yb, k8, turn, p6, sl 1, yf, turn, sl 1, yb, k6, turn, p4, sl 1, yf, turn, sl 1, yb, k4, turn, cast off 27 sts, p to end. 56 sts.
Next row K2 tog, k25, m1, k2, m1, k25, k2 tog.
Dec one st at each end of next 2 rows. 52 sts. Work 27 rows straight.
Shape Front Legs
Next row Cast on 30 sts, k55, m1, k2, m1, k25.
Cast on 30 sts at beg of next row. 114 sts. Work 2 rows.
Next row K56, m1, k2, m1, k56.
Work 3 rows.
Next row K57, m1, k2, m1, k57.
Work 1 row.
Next row K58, m1, k2, m1, k58.
Work 1 row.

Next row K59, m1, k2, m1, k59.
Work 1 row.
Next row K8, yf, sl 1, yb, turn, sl 1, p8, turn, k6, yf, sl 1, yb, turn, sl 1, p6, turn, k4, yf, sl 1, yb, turn, sl 1, p4, turn, cast off 30 sts, k29 sts more, m1, k2, m1, k60.
Next row P8, sl 1, yf, turn, sl 1, yb, k8, turn, p6, sl 1, yf, turn, sl 1, yb, k6, turn, p4, sl 1, yf, turn, sl 1, yb, k4, turn, cast off 30 sts, p30 sts more, m1, p2, m1, p31. 66 sts.
Shape Neck
Next row K33, turn; leave rem sts on a holder.
Work on first set of sts only. Cast on 17 sts at beg of next row.
Next row K2 tog, k to last st, k twice in last st.
Work 1 row. Rep last 2 rows once more.
Next row K2 tog, k to last st, k twice in last st.
Next row P to last 2 sts, p2 tog.
Rep last 2 rows once more.
Next row Cast off 5 sts, k to last 7 sts, slip these 7 sts onto a safety pin for head gusset.
Work 1 row. Cast off 5 sts at beg of next row and 9 sts at beg of foll alt row, marking centre st of the 9 cast off sts. Work 1 row.
Next row Cast off 6 sts, k to last 2 sts, k2 tog. 15 sts.

Shape Head
Work 3 rows.
Next row K8, k2 tog, k3, k2 tog.
Work 3 rows.
Next row K2 tog, k5, k2 tog, k2, k2 tog.
Work 5 rows. Mark end of last row.
Dec one st at end of next row and foll 6th row, then at each end of foll row. Cast off rem 4 sts.
With right side facing, rejoin yarn at inside edge to sts on a holder, cast on 17 sts, k to end. Work 1 row.
Next row K twice in first st, k to last 2 sts, k2 tog.
Rep last 2 rows once more. Work 1 row.
Next row K twice in first st, k to last 2 sts, k2 tog.
Next row P2 tog, p to end.
Rep last 2 rows once more.
Next row K7 and slip these sts onto a safety pin for head gusset, k to end.
Cast off 5 sts at beg of next row and foll alt row, then 9 sts at beg of foll alt row, marking centre st of the 9 cast off sts.
Dec one st at beg of next row. Cast off 6 sts at beg of next row. 15 sts.
Shape Head
Work 2 rows.
Next row K2 tog, k3, skpo, k8.
Work 3 rows.
Next row K2 tog, k2, skpo, k5, k2 tog.
Work 5 rows. Mark beg of last row.

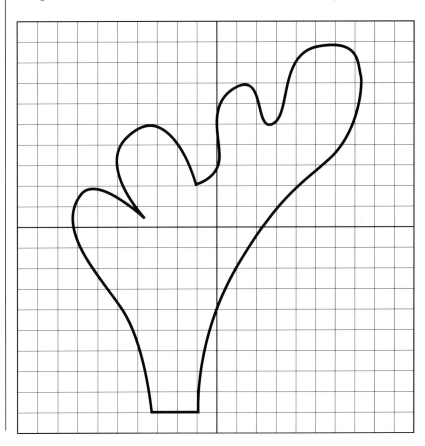

Dec one st at each end of next row and foll 6th row, then at each end of foll row. Cast off rem 4 sts.

Front Gusset

Place sts from safety pins on top of head onto one needle. With right side facing, rejoin yarn and k6, k2 tog, k6. 13 sts. Cont in st st, dec one st at each end of 10th row and 3 foll 4th rows. Work 11 rows straight. Dec one st at each end of next row. Work 3 rows. Work 3 tog and fasten off.

UNDERSIDE

Cast on 3 sts. Mark centre st. Beg with a k row, work in st st, inc one st at each end of 5 foll 3rd rows. 13 sts. Work 7 rows straight. Mark each end of last row.

Shape Back Legs

Cast on 5 sts at beg of next 2 rows.
Next row Cast on 5 sts, k9, skpo, k11, k2 tog, k4.
Cast on 5 sts at beg of next row.
Next row Cast on 20 sts, k29, skpo, k9, k2 tog, k9.
Cast on 20 sts at beg of next row. 69 sts.
Next row K29, skpo, k7, k2 tog, k29.
Work 1 row.
Next row K29, skpo, k5, k2 tog, k29.
Work 1 row.
Next row K29, skpo, k3, k2 tog, k29.
Work 3 rows.
Next row K30, m1, k3, m1, k30.
Work 1 row.

Next row K30, m1, k5, m1, k30.
Work 1 row.
Next row K8, yf, sl 1, yb, turn, sl 1, p8, turn, k6, yf, sl 1, yb, turn, sl 1, p6, turn, k4, yf, sl 1, yb, turn, sl 1, p4, turn, cast off 27 sts, k2 sts more, m1, k7, m1, k30.
Next row P8, sl 1, yf, turn, sl 1, yb, k8, turn, p6, sl 1, yf, turn, sl 1, yb, k6, turn, p4, sl 1, yf, turn, sl 1, yb, k4, turn, cast off 27 sts, p to end.
Next row K2 tog, k1, m1, k9, m1, k1, k2 tog.
Dec one st at each end of next row.
Next row K2 tog, m1, k9, m1, k2 tog.
13 sts. Inc one st at each end of 2 foll 4th rows. Work 11 rows straight. Dec one st at each end of next row and foll 4th row. Work 3 rows.

Shape Front Legs

Cast on 30 sts at beg of next 2 rows. 73 sts.
Next row K29, skpo, k11, k2 tog, k29.
Work 1 row.
Next row K29, skpo, k9, k2 tog, k29.
Work 1 row.
Next row K29, skpo, k7, k2 tog, k29.
Work 1 row.
Next row K29, skpo, k5, k2 tog, k29.
Work 1 row.
Next row K30, m1, k5, m1, k30.
Work 1 row.
Next row K30, m1, k7, m1, k30.
Work 1 row.
Next row K8, yf, sl 1, yb, turn, sl 1, p8, turn, k6, yf, sl 1, yb, turn, sl 1, p6, turn,

k4, yf, sl 1, yb, turn, sl 1, p4, turn, cast off 30 sts (1 st on needle), m1, k7, m1, k31.
Next row P8, sl 1, yf, turn, sl 1, yb, k8, turn, p6, sl 1, yf, turn, sl 1, yb, k6, turn, p4, sl 1, yf, turn, sl 1, yb, k4, turn, cast off 30 sts, p to end. 11 sts.
Dec one st at each end of 5th row and 3 foll 6th rows. Work 3 rows. Work 3 tog and fasten off.

EARS (make 4)

Cast on 10 sts. Work in st st, dec one st at each end of 7th row and 3 foll alt rows. Work 1 row. Work 2 tog and fasten off.

TAIL

Cast on 15 sts. K 2 rows. Cast off.

TO MAKE UP

Join back neck seam and front neck seam between markers. Sew in head gusset. Sew underside to upper body, matching legs and markers and leaving an opening. Stuff firmly and close opening. Join paired ear pieces together and sew them in place. Sew on tail. Trace antler from diagram onto felt and cut out 4 pieces. Oversew 2 pieces together stuffing firmly as you sew. Sew antlers in place. With Black, embroider nostrils and mouth. Embroider eyes with Black and White yarn.

Mother and Baby Kangaroo

See Page
37

MATERIALS
Mother 3×50g balls of Rowan Designer DK Wool in main colour (A) and 1 ball in contrast colour (B).
Baby 1×50g ball of Rowan Designer DK Wool in main colour (A) and small amount of same in contrast colour (B).

Oddment of Black yarn for embroidery.
Pair of 3¼mm (No 10/US 3) knitting needles.
Stuffing.

MEASUREMENTS
Mother Approximately 41cm/16in high.
Baby Approximately 14cm/5½in high.

TENSION
28 sts and 36 rows to 10cm/4in square over st st.

ABBREVIATIONS
See page 10.

Mother

LEFT SIDE PANEL
Tail
With A, cast on 59 sts. K 1 row.
Next row P twice in first st, p to end.
Next row K to last st, k twice in last st.
Rep last 2 rows once more, then work first of the 2 rows again. 64 sts.
Next row Cast off 8 sts, k to last st, k twice in last st.
Next row P twice in first st, p to end.
Next row Cast off 6 sts, k to end.
Next row Cast on 3 sts, p to end.
Mark beg of last row. Cont in st st, casting off 6 sts at beg of next row, 4 sts at beg of 4 foll alt rows, then 3 sts at beg of foll alt row. 30 sts. Leave these sts on a holder.
Foot
** With A, cast on 30 sts. K 1 row.
Next row [P1, m1] twice, p to last 2 sts, [m1, p1] twice. 34 sts.
Beg with a k row, work 10 rows in st st.
Dec one st at end of next row and at same edge on 2 foll rows. Cast off 3 sts at beg of next row and 13 sts at beg of foll alt row. 15 sts. ** Work 3 rows in st st.
Body
Next row P to end, then p across sts on a holder. 45 sts.
Cont in st st, inc one st at end of next row and 4 foll 4th rows. 50 sts. Work 3 rows straight. Dec one st at end of next row and foll 4th row, then on 4 foll alt rows. Dec one st at beg of next row. 43 sts.
Next row K20, skpo, k to last 2 sts, k2 tog.

Dec one st at beg of next row and at end of foll row. 39 sts. Work 1 row.
Shape Body
1st row Skpo, k18, skpo, k17.
Work 3 rows.
5th row K19, skpo, k16.
Work 1 row.
7th row Skpo, k to end.
Work 1 row.
9th row K18, skpo, k15.
Work 3 rows.
13th row Skpo, k16, skpo, k14.
Work 3 rows.
17th row K17, skpo, k13.
Work 1 row.
19th row As 7th row.
Work 1 row.
21st row K16, skpo, k12.
Work 3 rows.
25th row Skpo, k14, skpo, k11.
Work 3 rows.
29th row K15, skpo, k10.
Work 1 row.
31st row As 7th row.
Work 1 row.
33rd row K14, skpo, k9.
Work 3 rows.
37th row Skpo, k12, skpo, k8.
Work 3 rows.
41st row K13, skpo, k7.
Work 1 row.
43rd row As 7th row.
Work 1 row.
45th row K12, skpo, k6.
Work 3 rows.
49th row K12, skpo, k5. 18 sts.
Work 2 rows.
Shape Head
Cast on 4 sts at beg of next row and 8 sts at beg of foll alt row. Mark 1st and 4th sts of the 8 cast on sts. Inc one st at end of next row and at same edge on 2 foll rows. 33 sts. Work 7 rows.
Dec one st at end of next row and at same edge on 4 foll rows. Cast off 9 sts at beg of next row and 4 sts at beg of foll alt row, then 8 sts at beg of foll alt row. Leave rem 7 sts on a holder.

RIGHT SIDE PANEL
Work as given for Left Side Panel, reversing shapings by reading p for k and k for p and working p2 tog instead of skpo when shaping.

RIGHT INSIDE FOOT
Work as given for Left Side Panel from ** to **. Work 2 rows in st st. Cast off 4 sts at beg of next row. Work 1 row. Mark end of last row. Inc one st at end of next row. Work 3 rows.
Next row K2 tog, k to last st, k twice in last st.
Rep last 4 rows 3 times more. Work 3 rows. Dec one st at end of next row and foll 4th row, then on 4 foll alt rows. Now dec one st at beg of next row and at same edge on 3 foll rows. Work 2 tog and fasten off.

LEFT INSIDE FOOT
Work as given for Right Inside Foot, reversing shapings by reading p for k and k for p.

CENTRE PANEL
*** With B, cast on 18 sts. Beg with a k row, work in st st, dec one st at each end of 2 foll alt rows. 14 sts. Work 2 rows. Mark each end of last row. ***
Inc one st at each end of next row and 8 foll 4th rows. 32 sts. Dec one st at each end of 2nd row and every foll 4th row until 2 sts rem. Work 2 tog and fasten off.

POUCH
Work as given for Centre Panel from *** to ***.
Next row K twice in first st, k2, [m1, k2] 5 times, k twice in last st. 21 sts.
Inc one st at each end of 6 foll 4th rows and 3 foll alt rows. 39 sts. Work 2 rows. Cast off knitwise.

LEFT OUTER ARM
With A, cast on 22 sts. K 1 row.
Next row [P1, m1] twice, p to last 2 sts, [m1, p1] twice.
Work 8 rows in st st.
Next row K twice in first st, k to last 2 sts, k2 tog.
Dec one st at beg of next row and at end of foll row. Cast off 15 sts at beg of next row. Inc one st at beg of next row. Work 1 row. Inc one st at end of next row. Work 1 row. Inc one st at each end of next row. Work 7 rows. Dec one st at each end of next row and foll alt row, then on foll row. 7 sts. Cast off.

RIGHT INNER ARM
Work as given for Left Outer Arm.

RIGHT OUTER AND LEFT INNER ARMS
Work as given for Left Outer Arm, reversing shapings by reading p for k and k for p.

EARS (make 4)
With A, cast on 19 sts.
Next 2 rows K3, sl 1, turn, yb, sl 1, yf, p to end.
Next 2 rows K5, sl 1, turn, yb, sl 1, yf, p to end.
Next 2 rows K7, sl 1, turn, yb, sl 1, yf, p to end.
K 1 row across all sts.
Next 2 rows P3, sl 1, yb, turn, sl 1, yb, k to end.
Next 2 rows P5, sl 1, yb, turn, sl 1, yb, k to end.
Next 2 rows P7, sl 1, yb, turn, sl 1, yb, k to end.
Next row P8, p twice in next st, [m1, p twice in next st] twice, p8.
24 sts. Work 4 rows in st st.
Next row K10, skpo, k2 tog, k10.

Work 3 rows.
Next row K9, skpo, k2 tog, k9.
Work 1 row. Dec one st at each end of next row and 4 foll alt rows, then on every row until 2 sts rem. P2 tog and fasten off.

TOP HEAD PANEL
Place top sts of side panels on one needle. With right side facing and A, k6, k2 tog, k6. 13 sts. Beg with a p row, work in st st, dec one st at each end of 5 foll 8th rows. Work 3 rows. K3 tog and fasten off.

TO MAKE UP
Join back seam of side panels and bottom seam of tail to markers. Join head pieces together between markers. Sew top head panel in place.
Sew inside feet to outside feet of side panels. Place pouch on top of lower part of centre panel, join row end edges and cast on edges together. Stitch cast on edge of centre panel to row ends of tail part of side panels. Sew centre panel in place, matching markers and leaving an opening. Stuff and close opening. Join paired arm pieces together, leaving an opening. Stuff and close opening. Sew arms in place. Join paired ear pieces together. Fold cast on edge in half, secure and sew in place. With Black, embroider eyes, nostrils and mouth.

Baby

LEFT SIDE PANEL
Tail
With A, cast on 19 sts. K 1 row.
Next row P twice in next st, p to end.
Next row Cast off 6 sts, k to last st, k twice in last st.
Cont in st st, cast on 2 sts at beg of next row. Mark beg of last row. Cast off 4 sts at beg of next row and 3 sts at beg of foll alt row. 10 sts. Work 2 rows. Leave these sts on a holder.

Foot
** With A, cast on 10 sts. K 1 row.
Next row P twice in first st, p to last st, p twice in last st.
Cont in st st, work 3 rows. Dec one st at beg of next row and at end of foll row. Cast off 4 sts at beg of foll row. 6 sts. **
Work 1 row.

Body
Next row P to end, then p across sts on a holder. 16 sts.
Cont in st st, inc one st at end of next

row and 2 foll alt rows. 19 sts. Work 2 rows. Dec one st at beg of next row and foll alt row.
Next row Skpo, k13, k2 tog.
P 1 row. Mark beg of last row.
Shape Body
1st row Skpo, k13.
2nd row and every foll alt row P.
3rd row K6, skpo, k6.
5th row Skpo, k11.
7th row K5, skpo, k5.
9th row Skpo, k9.
11th row K4, skpo, k4.
13th row Skpo, k7.
15th row K3, skpo, k3.
17th row Skpo, k5. 6 sts.
Work 2 rows.
Shape Head
Cast on 2 sts at beg of next row. Work 1 row. Mark end of last row. Cast on 3 sts at beg of next row. Mark beg of last row. Work 2 rows. Dec one st at end of next row. Cast off 3 sts at beg of foll row. Rep last 2 rows once. Leave rem 3 sts on a holder.

RIGHT SIDE PANEL
Work as given for Left Side Panel, reversing shapings by reading p for k and k for p and working p2 tog instead of skpo when shaping.

RIGHT INSIDE FOOT
Work as given for Left Side Panel from ** to **. Cast off 2 sts at beg of next row. Work 1 row. Mark end of last row. Inc one st at end of next row. Dec one st at end of next row. Inc one st at end of next row. Work 1 row.
Next row K2 tog, k2, k twice in last st. Work 2 rows. Dec one st at beg of next row and foll alt row. Dec one st at end of next row. P 1 row. K2 tog and fasten off.

LEFT INSIDE FOOT
Work as given for Right Inside Foot, reversing shapings by reading p for k and k for p.

CENTRE PANEL
With B, cast on 6 sts. Beg with a k row, work in st st, dec one st at each end of 3rd row. Mark each end of last row. Work 2 rows. Inc one st at each end of next row and 3 foll alt rows. 12 sts. Work 4 rows. Mark each end of last row. Dec one st at each end of next row and 4 foll 4th rows. 2 sts. P 1 row. K2 tog and fasten off.

LEFT OUTER ARM
With A, cast on 7 sts. K 1 row.

Next row P twice in first st, p5, p twice in last st.
K 1 row.
Next row P2 tog, p6, p twice in last st.
Next row K7, k2 tog.
Next row Cast off 5 sts, p1 st more, p twice in last st.
Next row K3, k twice in last st.
Inc one st at beg of next row. Work 1 row. Dec one st at end of next row. Dec one st at each end of next row. Cast off rem 3 sts.

RIGHT INNER ARM
Work as given for Left Outer Arm.

RIGHT OUTER AND LEFT INNER ARMS
Work as given for Left Outer Arm, reversing shaping by reading p for k and k for p.

EARS (make 4)
With A, cast on 6 sts.
Next 2 rows K1, sl 1, turn, yb, sl 1, yf, p1.
Next 2 rows K2, sl 1, turn, yb, sl 1, yf, p2.
K across all sts.
Next 2 rows P1, sl 1, yb, turn, sl 1, yb, k1.
Next 2 rows P2, sl 1, yb, turn, sl 1, yb, k2.
P across all sts.
Next row K2, [k twice in next st] twice, k2.
P 1 row.
Next row K2, skpo, k2 tog, k2.
Dec one st at each end of 2 foll alt rows.
P 1 row. K2 tog and fasten off.

TOP HEAD PANEL
Place top sts of side panels on one needle. With right side facing and A, k2, k2 tog, k2. 5 sts. Beg with a p row, work in st st, dec one st at each end of 6th row. Work 5 rows. K 3 tog and fasten off.

TO MAKE UP
Join back seam of side panels and bottom seam of tail to markers. Join head pieces together between markers. Sew top head panel in place. Sew inside feet to outside feet of side panels. Stitch cast on edge of centre panel to row ends of tail part of side panels. Sew centre panel in place, matching markers and leaving an opening. Stuff and close opening.
Join paired arm pieces together, stuffing as you sew. Sew arms in place.
Join paired ear pieces together. Fold cast on edge in half, secure and sew in place. With Black, embroider eyes, nostrils and mouth.

Monkey

See Page
38

MATERIALS
1×50g ball of Rowan Designer DK Wool in Brown (A) and small amount in Beige (B).
1×50g ball of Rowan Handknit DK Cotton in Red (C).
Oddments of Black yarn and Gold lurex yarn.
Pair of 3¼mm (No 10/US 3) knitting needles.
Stuffing.

MEASUREMENTS
Monkey Approximately 18cm/7in high.

TENSION
28 sts and 36 rows to 10cm/4in square over st st.

ABBREVIATIONS
See page 10.

Monkey

LEGS (make 2)
With A, cast on 13 sts. Beg with a k row, work 16 rows in st st.
Next row K1, [skpo, k1, k2 tog, k1] twice.
P 1 row.
Next row K1, [k2 tog] to end.
Break off yarn, thread end through rem sts, pull up and secure.
Join seam, leaving cast on edge free. Stuff legs.

FEET (make 2)
With B, cast on 8 sts. Beg with a p row, work 5 rows in st st.
Next row K5, turn.
Work 3 rows on these 5 sts. Cast off.
With right side facing, rejoin yarn to rem sts and work 2 rows.
K3 tog and fasten off.
With B, cast on 8 sts. Beg with a p row, work 5 rows in st st.
Next row K3, turn.
Work 1 row on these 3 sts. K3 tog and fasten off.
With right side facing, rejoin yarn to rem sts and work 4 rows. Cast off.
With paired pieces together, join seam around edges. Place open end of legs on top of feet and sew in position.

BODY
Begin at neck edge.
With A, cast on 15 sts. P 1 row.
Next row K1, [m1, k1] to end. 29 sts.
Beg with a p row, work 5 rows in st st.
Next row [K7, m1] twice, k1, [m1, k7] twice.
Work 3 rows.
Next row K16, m1, k1, m1, k16. 35 sts.
Work 5 rows.

Next row K15, skpo, k1, k2 tog, k15.
Work 3 rows.
Next row K14, skpo, k1, k2 tog, k14.
Work 3 rows.
Next row K1, [k2 tog] to end. 16 sts.
P 1 row. Cast off.

ARMS (make 2)
With A, cast on 13 sts. Beg with a k row, work 20 rows in st st.
Next row K1, [skpo, k1, k2 tog, k1] twice.
P 1 row.
Next row K1, [k2 tog] to end.
Break off yarn, thread end through rem sts, pull up and secure. Join seam, leaving cast on edge free. Stuff arms.

HANDS (make 2)
Work as given for Feet, but leaving cast on edges of hands open. Sew open edges of hands to open edges of arms.

HEAD
Begin at neck edge.
With A, cast on 7 sts. P 1 row.
Next row K1, [m1, k1] to end.
Rep last 2 rows once more. Work 3 rows in st st.
Next row K1, [m1, k3] to end. 33 sts.
Work 9 rows.
Next row K1, [k2 tog, k2] to end.
P 1 row.
Next row K1, [k2 tog, k1] to end.
P 1 row.
Next row K1, [k2 tog] to end.
Break off yarn, thread end through rem sts, pull up and secure.
Join seam, leaving an opening. Stuff firmly and close opening.

MUZZLE
With B, cast on 12 sts for underchin. Beg with a k row, work 4 rows in st st.
Dec one st at each end of next row and foll alt row, then at each end of foll 2 rows. Cast off rem 4 sts.
With B, cast on 4 sts for main part. Beg with a k row, work in st st, inc one st at each end of 2nd row and 2 foll rows, then at each end of foll alt row.
Next row K4, skpo, k2 tog, k4.
Next row P3, p2 tog, p2 tog tbl, p3. 8 sts.
Mark each end of last row. K 1 row. Inc one st at each end of next 2 rows.
P 1 row.
Next 2 rows K5, yf, sl 1, yb, turn, sl 1, p4, sl 1.
Next row K to end.
Next 2 rows P5, sl 1, yb, turn, sl 1, yb, k4, yf, sl 1.
Next row P5, cast off next 2 sts, p to end.
Cast off first 5 sts. Rejoin yarn to rem 5 sts, cast off these sts.
With right sides together and with cast on edge of underchin in line with markers on main part, join "mouth" seam. Turn to

right side and stuff lower part of muzzle. Sew in place.

EARS (make 4)
With B, cast on 6 sts. Work in st st, inc one st at each end of 2nd row.
Work 4 rows straight. Dec one st at each end of next 2 rows. Cast off.

TAIL
With A, cast on 20 sts. Work 4 rows in st st. Cast off.

TO MAKE UP
Fold sides of cast off edge of body to centre and sew it together, then join back seam. Stuff body firmly. Gather neck edge, pull up and secure. Sew on head, arms and legs in place. Join paired ear pieces together and sew them in place. Fold tail widthwise and stitch together folded edges. Sew tail in place. With A, embroider eyes and top of nose.

Waistcoat

BACK AND FRONTS
With C, cast on 16 sts. K 13 rows.
Shape Armholes
Next row Cast off 3, k to end.
Rep last row once more. 10 sts. K 10 rows.
Shape Neck
Next row K3, cast off next 4 sts, k to end.
Cont on last set of sts for Left Front. K 2 rows.
Next row K to last st, k twice in last st.
K 1 row. Rep last 2 rows once more. 5 sts. K 6 rows.
Next row Cast on 3 sts, k to end.
K 13 rows on these 8 sts. Cast off.
Rejoin yarn at inside edge to rem sts and k to end. K 1 row.
Next row K twice in first st, k to end.
Rep last 2 rows once more. 5 sts.
K 6 rows.
Next row Cast on 3 sts, k to end.
K 14 rows on these 8 sts. Cast off.

TO MAKE UP
Join side seams. With length of lurex yarn, work a row of back stitches around lower edge, front edges and back neck.

Fez

With C, cast on 10 sts for brim. Work 4 rows in st st. Cast off. Join seam.
With C, cast on 3 sts for top. K 1 row.
Next row P1, p twice in next st, p1.
Work 2 rows in st st.
Next row K1, k2 tog, k1.
P 1 row. Cast off.
Sew top to brim. With Black, make small tassel and attach to top of fez.
Sew fez to top of Monkey head.

Camel

See Page
39

MATERIALS
3 × 25g hanks of Rowan Lightweight DK in Brown (A).
Small amount of DK Cotton in each of Cream (B), Red (C), Wine (D), Blue (E), Green (F), Brick (G) and Pink (H).
Oddments of Black and White yarn for embroidery.
Pair each of 3¼mm (No 10/US 3) and 4mm (No 8/US 5) knitting needles.
Medium size crochet hook.
Stuffing.

MEASUREMENTS
Approximately 31cm/12in high and 28cm/11in long.

TENSION
28 sts and 36 rows to 10cm/4in square over st st on 3¼mm (No 10/US 3) needles.

ABBREVIATIONS
See page 10.

Camel

UPPER BODY
Right Back Leg
With 3¼mm (No 10/US 3) needles and A, cast on 3 sts. P 1 row.
Next row Cast on 4 sts, k to end.
P 1 row.
Next row Cast on 4 sts, k to last st, m1, k1.
P 1 row. Rep last 2 rows twice more. 22 sts.
Next row Cast on 24 sts, k10, turn, p5, turn, k8, turn, p10, turn, k to last st, m1, k1. 47 sts.
Leave these sts on a holder.

Left Back Leg
With 3¼mm (No 10/US 3) needles and A, cast on 3 sts. K 1 row.
Next row Cast on 4 sts, p to end.
Next row K1, m1, k to end.
Rep last 2 rows 3 times more. 23 sts.
Next row Cast on 24 sts, p10, turn, k5, turn, p8, turn, k10, turn, p to end, then p across sts of Right Back Leg. 94 sts.
Mark centre of last row.
Next row K to within 1 st of centre, m1, k2, m1, k to end.
P 1 row. Rep last 2 rows once.
Next row K to within 1 st of centre, m1, k2, m1, k to end.
Next row P to within 1 st of centre, m1, p2, m1, p to end.
Rep last 2 rows 3 times.
Next row K6, turn, p6, turn, k4, turn, p4, turn, k2, turn, p2, turn, cast off 27 sts, k to within 1 st of centre, m1, k2, m1, k to

end.
Next row P6, turn, k6, turn, p4, turn, k4, turn, p2, turn, k2, turn, cast off 27 sts, p to within 1 st of centre, m1, p2, m1, p to end. 64 sts.
Next row K2 tog, k29, m1, k2, m1, k29, k2 tog.
Next row P2 tog, p29, m1, p2, m1, p29, p2 tog.
Next row K2 tog, k29, m1, k2, m1, k29, k2 tog.
Next row P2 tog, p to last 2 sts, p2 tog.
Next row K to within 1 st of centre, m1, k2, m1, k to end.
P 1 row. Rep last 2 rows twice more. 68 sts. Work 4 rows straight.
Next row K to within 3 sts of centre, k2 tog, k2, skpo, k to end.
P 1 row. Rep last 2 rows once more.
Next row K to within 3 sts of centre, k2 tog, k2, skpo, k to end.
Next row P to within 3 sts of centre, p2 tog tbl, p2, p2 tog, p to end.
Rep last 2 rows once more. 56 sts.
Shape Front Legs
Next row Cast on 27 sts, k52, k2 tog, k2, skpo, k to end.
Next row Cast on 27 sts, p51, p2 tog tbl, p2, p2 tog, p to end.
Next row K twice in first st, k to within 3 sts of centre, k2 tog, k2, skpo, k to last st, k twice in last st.
Next row P twice in first st, p to within 3 sts of centre, p2 tog tbl, p2, p2 tog, p to last st, p twice in last st.
Rep last 2 rows once. 106 sts.
Next row K to within 3 sts of centre, k2 tog, k2, skpo, k to end.
P 1 row. Rep last 2 rows twice more. 100 sts. Work 2 rows straight.
Next row K6, turn, p6, turn, k4, turn, p4, turn, k2, turn, p2, turn, cast off 30 sts, k to end.
Next row P6, turn, k6, turn, p4, turn, k4, turn, p2, turn, k2, turn, cast off 30 sts, p to end. 40 sts.
Shape Neck
Work 2 rows straight. Dec one st at each end of next row. Work 1 row.
Next row K18, m1, k2, m1, k18.
Work 3 rows.
Next row K2 tog, k17, m1, k2, m1, k17, k2 tog.
Work 1 row.
Next row K19, m1, k2, m1, k19.
Next row P20, m1, p2, m1, p20.
Next row K2 tog, k19, m1, k2, m1, k19, k2 tog.
Next row P21, m1, p2, m1, p21.
Next row K2 tog, k21, turn.
Work on this set of sts only.
Next row Cast on 3 sts, p to end.
Next row K2 tog, k to end.
Next row Cast on 3 sts, p to end.
Mark end of last row.
Next row Cast off 4 sts, k to end.
Shape Head
Next row Cast on 15 sts, p to end. Mark centre st of the 15 cast on sts.

Next row Cast off 3 sts, k to last st, k twice in last st.
Next row P twice in first st, p to end.
Next row Cast off 3 sts, k to last st, k twice in last st.
P 1 row. Cast off 3 sts at beg of next row and foll alt row.
****Work 1 row. Cast off 11 sts at beg of next row. Dec one st at end of next row and at same edge on 2 foll rows. Dec one st at end of next row and 2 foll alt rows. Work 2 rows. Dec one st at end of next row. Work 3 rows. Dec one st at each end of next row. Dec one st at end of next row and at each end of foll 2 rows. Mark centre of last row. Cast off.
With right side facing, rejoin yarn to rem sts.
Next row Cast on 3 sts, k to last 2 sts, k2 tog.
P 1 row. Rep last 2 rows once.
Shape Head
Cast on 15 sts at beg of next row. Mark centre st of the 15 cast on sts.
Next row Cast off 4 sts, p to last st, p twice in last st.
Next row K twice in first st, k to end.
Next row Cast off 3 sts, p to last st, p twice in last st.
Work 1 row. Cast off 3 sts at beg of next row and 2 foll alt rows.
Work as given for first side from ** to end.

UNDERSIDE
With 3¼mm (No 10/US 3) needles and A, cast on 25 sts. Mark centre st.
Beg with a k row, work 2 rows in st st.
Cast on 4 sts at beg of next 2 rows.
Next row Cast on 4 sts, k18, skpo, k1, k2 tog, k to end.
Cast on 4 sts at beg of next row.
Next row Cast on 4 sts, k21, skpo, k1, k2 tog, k to end.
Cast on 4 sts at beg of next row.
Next row Cast on 24 sts, k10, turn, p5, turn, k8, turn, p10, turn, k28, k2 tog, k11, skpo, k1, k2 tog, k11, skpo, k to end.
Next row Cast on 24 sts, p10, turn, k5, turn, p8, turn, k10, turn, p to end.
Next row K31, k2 tog, k9, skpo, k1, k2 tog, k9, skpo, k31.
P 1 row.
Next row K31, k2 tog, k7, skpo, k1, k2 tog, k7, skpo, k31.
P 1 row.
Next row K31, k2 tog, k5, skpo, k1, k2 tog, k5, skpo, k31.
P 1 row.
Next row K31, k2 tog, k3, skpo, k1, k2 tog, k3, skpo, k31.
P 1 row.
Next row K31, [k2 tog, k1, skpo, k1] twice, k30.
P 1 row.
Next row K31, m1, k1, skpo, k1, k2 tog, k1, m1, k31.
P 1 row.
Next row K6, turn, p6, turn, k4, turn, p4,

turn, k2, turn, p2, turn, cast off 27 sts, k3 sts more, m1, k7, m1, k to end.
Next row P6, turn, k6, turn, p4, turn, k4, turn, p2, turn, k2, turn, cast off 27 sts, p 3 sts more, m1, p9, m1, p to end.
Next row K2 tog, k2, m1, k11, m1, k2, k2 tog.
Next row P2 tog, p1, m1, p13, m1, p1, p2 tog.
Next row K2 tog, k15, k2 tog.
Next row P2 tog, p to last 2 sts, p2 tog. 15 sts.
Work 4 rows. Dec one st at each end of next row. Work 7 rows. Inc one st at each end of next row. Work 5 rows.
Next row Cast on 27 sts, k27, [skpo] twice, k7, [k2 tog] twice.
Cast on 27 sts at beg of next row.
Next row K twice in first st, k26, skpo, k7, k2 tog, k26, k twice in last st.
Next row P twice in first st, p to last st, p twice in last st.
Next row K twice in first st, k28, skpo, k5, k2 tog, k28, k twice in last st.
Inc one st at each end of next row.
Next row K31, skpo, k3, k2 tog, k31.
Work 3 rows.
Next row K32, m1, k3, m1, k32.
P 1 row.
Next row K32, m1, k5, m1, k32.
P 1 row.
Next row K6, turn, p6, turn, k4, turn, p4, turn, k2, turn, p2, turn, cast off 30 sts, k1 st more, m1, k7, m1, k to end.
Next row P6, turn, k6, turn, p4, turn, k4, turn, p2, turn, k2, turn, cast off 30 sts, p1 st more, m1, p9, m1, p to end. 15 sts.
Work 8 rows. Dec one st at each end of next row, foll 4th row, foll alt row, then on every row until 3 sts rem. Work 3 tog and fasten off.

HEAD GUSSET

Begin at back. With 3¼mm (No 10/US 3) needles and A, cast on 3 sts. Beg with a k row, work in st st, inc one st at each end of every alt row until there are 13 sts.

Work 7 rows. Dec one st at each end of next row and foll alt row. Work 9 rows. Inc one st at each end of next row and foll alt row. Work 1 row. Dec one st at each end of every row until 3 sts rem. Work 3 tog and fasten off.

BACK SOLES (make 2)

Begin at back. With 3¼mm (No 10/US 3) needles and A, cast on 3 sts. Work in st st, inc one st at each end of every alt row until there are 11 sts. Work 3 rows. Cast off 2 sts at beg of next 4 rows. Cast off rem 3 sts.

FRONT SOLES (make 2)

Begin at back. With 3¼mm (No 10/US 3) needles and A, cast on 3 sts. Work in st st, inc one st at each end of every alt row until there are 9 sts. Work 1 row. Cast off 2 sts at beg of next 2 rows. Cast off rem 5 sts.

EARS (make 2)

With 3¼mm (No 10/US 3) needles and A, cast on 11 sts. Work 4 rows in st st. Dec one st at each end of every row until 3 sts rem. Work 3 tog and fasten off.

TAIL

With 3¼mm (No 10/US 3) needles and A, cast on 25 sts. Work 6 rows in st st. Cast off.

TO MAKE UP

Join back neck seam of upper body to markers, then join seam between markers of front neck and underchin. Sew in head gusset. Join underside to body, matching markers and legs and leaving an opening and ends of legs free. Sew in soles. Stuff firmly and close opening. Fold tail widthwise and join together long edges. Sew tail in place. Fold ears in half and sew cast on edge in place. With Black, embroider mouth. Embroider eyes with Black and White yarn.

Blanket

With 4mm (No 8/US 5) needles and B, cast on 16 sts.
1st row (right side) P to end.
2nd row P2, k12, p2.
With C, rep 1st and 2nd rows once. With D, rep 1st and 2nd rows once. With E, rep 1st and 2nd rows once. With F, rep 1st and 2nd rows once. With B, rep 1st and 2nd rows once. Rep last 10 rows 3 times more. With B, cast off.
Make 4 small tassels in each of C, E, F and H. Attach tassels to blanket in 4 rows as shown on photograph alternating colours.

Saddle Pommel

With 4mm (No 8/US 5) needles and G, cast on 50 sts. Cast off.
Loop under first and last 8 sts and sew down. Place pommel on Camel, leaving doubled ends pointing upwards. Secure in position. Place blanket on top and secure in position.

Reins

With crochet hook and G, make chain approximately 50cm/20in long. Join ends. Loop round nose and secure in position. With G, make another crochet chain approximately 20cm/8in long. Place this chain around head attaching ends to nose band. Secure in place. Make few tassels in C, E, F and H colours. Attach tassels to chain at each side of head alternating colours.

Yarn Source Guide

Rowan Yarn Addresses
Rowan Yarns are widely available in yarn shops. For details of stockists and mail order sources of Rowan yarns, please write or contact the distributors listed below. For advice on substitute yarns, see page 10.

UNITED KINGDOM
Rowan Yarns,
Green Lane Mill, Holmfirth, West Yorkshire, England
HD7 1RE.
Tel: (01484) 681 881

USA
Westminster Trading Corporation,
5 Northern Boulevard, Amherst, NH 03031.
Tel: (603) 886 5041/5043

AUSTRALIA
Rowan (Australia), 191 Canterbury Road, Canterbury, Victoria 3126.
Tel: (03) 830 1609

BELGIUM
Hedera, Pleinstraat 68, 3001 Leuven.
Tel: (016) 23 21 89

CANADA
Estelle Designs & Sales Ltd,
Unit 65 & 67, 2220 Midland Avenue, Scarborough, Ontario, M1P 3E6.
Tel: (416) 298 9922

DENMARK
Designer Garn, Vesterbro 33 A, DK-9000, Aalborg.
Tel: (8) 98 13 48 24

FRANCE
Sidel, Ch Depart, 14C 13840 Rognes.
Tel: (33) 42 50 15 06

GERMANY
Wolle + Design, Wolfshover Strasse 76, 52428 Julich-Stetiernich.
Tel: (02461) 54735

HOLLAND
Henk & Henrietta Beukers,
Dorpsstraat 9, NL-5327 AR, Hurwenen.
Tel: 04182 1764

ICELAND
Stockurinn, Kjorgardi, Laugavegi 59, ICE-101 Reykjavik.
Tel: (01) 18258

ITALY
La Compagnia del Cotone,
Via Mazzini 44, 1-10123 Torino.
Tel: (011) 87 83 81

JAPAN
Diakeito Co Ltd, 2-3-11 Senba-Higashi, Minoh City, Osaka 562.
Tel: 0727 27 6604

NEW ZEALAND
John Q Goldingham Ltd, PO Box 45083, Epuni Railway, Lower Hutt, Wellington, North Island.
Tel: (04) 5674 085

NORWAY
Eureka, PO Box 357, N-1401 Ski.
Tel: (64) 86 55 70

SWEDEN
Wincent, Sveavagen 94, 113 58 Stockholm.
Tel: (08) 673 70 60